HV
5132
.L395

30449100061293
Laybourn, Ann.
　 Hurting on the inside

HURTING ON THE INSIDE

Child - Ma Mum got hurt on the outside and we got hurt in the inside.

Father (in a different family) - It hurts me inside because I know how much it must have hurt him.

Hurting on the Inside

Children's Experiences of Parental Alcohol Misuse

ANN LAYBOURN
JANE BROWN
MALCOLM HILL

Avebury
Aldershot • Brookfield USA • Hong Kong • Singapore • Sydney

© A. Laybourn, Jane Brown and Malcolm Hill 1996

All rights reserved. No part of this publication may be reproduced, stored in a retrieval system, or transmitted in any form or by any means, electronic, mechanical, photocopying, recording or otherwise without the prior permission of the publisher.

Published by
Avebury
Ashgate Publishing Limited
Gower House
Croft Road
Aldershot
Hants GU11 3HR
England

Ashgate Publishing Company
Old Post Road
Brookfield
Vermont 05036
USA

A CIP catalogue record for this book is available from the British Library

ISBN 1 85972 319 5

Library of Congress Catalog Card Number: 96-84598

Printed and bound by Athenaeum Press, Ltd.,
Gateshead, Tyne & Wear.

Contents

Figures and tables vi
Acknowledgements vii
Preface viii

1. Alcohol, alcohol misuse and children — 1

2. Research design, methodological issues and fieldwork — 15

3. Problem drinking patterns — 36

4. The direct impact on the child — 43

5. Impact of the drinking on family dynamics with indirect consequences for the child — 62

6. Coping, support and communication — 75

7. Longer term implications of parental problem drinking — 94

8. Services - past, present and future — 100

9. Professional perspectives — 115

10. Summary and implications - reducing the hurt — 123

References 139

Appendix 1	Children's interview schedule	147
Appendix 2	Young adults' interview schedule	149
Appendix 3	Parents' interview schedule	153
Appendix 4	The impact of parental drinking on children	156

Subject Index 157
Author Index 163

Figures and tables

		Page
Table 2.1	Sources for the sample	22
Table 2.2	Characteristics of the sample	23
Table 2.3	Household types	24
Table 2.4	Gender of the identified problem drinker	25
Table 4.1	Children's responses to drunken behaviour	50

Acknowledgements

It is customary for researchers to thank people who have taken part in thier studies for giving their time and information. We are more than usually grateful to those who participated in our interviews, because they were willing to talk openly to strangers about matters which are often seen as especially private and shameful. Hence our greatest debt is to the children and parents who were willing to talk with us.

The study could not have taken place without the co-operation of a large number of individuals and agencies who took the trouble to help us in the difficult process of recruiting families for the study. Their commitment is much appreciated.

The research was funded jointly by the Health Education Board for Scotland and Barnardos Scotland. We value the support and guidance provided by the advisory group. Jonathan Watson of HEBS and Mike Hughes of Barnardos have given us great encouragement and provided helpful feedback on our findings and writings. The opinions expressed in this book are those of the authors, not the Health Education Board for Scotland nor Barnardos.

Neil McKeganey of the Drug Misuse Centre, University of Glasgow, provided valuable advice and support. Thanks are also due to Elaine Hodge and Laura Lochhead for their clerical assistance.

Preface

Participants who took part in the research on which this book is based were promised confidentiality. Therefore, when a name has been used in the text to refer to a participant in the study, a relative or friend, this has been changed from the original in order to disguise people's identity. As a number of children are referred to several times in the report, certain characteristics like gender or family composition (but not age) have occasionally been altered to preserve anonymity, although only when this 'disguise' has no major relevance to the topic under consideration.

All the quotations used in this book were reproduced verbatim from tape recordings of the interviews, apart from the alteration of names as indicated above. Occasionally a word is added in brackets to clarify the meaning. In the interests of authenticity, we have sought to reproduce the West of Scotland dialects of informants as closely as possible.

The word 'drinking' and the phrases 'heavy drinking' or 'alcohol misuse' are used in the book as a short-hand way of referring to heavy consumption of alcoholic drinks which seriously and repeatedly affects behaviour. The term 'identified drinker' (I.D.) is used to indicate the family member regarded as having a heavy drinking problem.

1 Alcohol, alcohol misuse and children

Introduction: The place of alcoholic drinks in society

Alcohol has perhaps a unique place in our culture as a widely used yet potentially addictive substance, which may be sold and consumed legally. Its position has become particularly distinctive now that smoking tobacco has become a minority activity, even if the minority is a substantial one. Unlike tobacco and drugs, alcoholic drinks are socially sanctioned, but when taken to excess they too can cause harm and even death to the drinker or others through their physiological effects and their contribution to violent behaviour and road accidents.

Present-day society in Britain and indeed in much of the modern world embraces two views of alcoholic drinks. On the one hand they are socially approved. In the UK about nine in ten adults regularly drink alcohol. It is the frequent accompaniment to meals and social gatherings, a recommended means of celebrating happy events like weddings, birthdays and sporting victories; and is readily available in pubs, bars, shops and restaurants.

On the other hand, alcoholic drinks are clearly acknowledged to be dangerous. They are thought to be unsuitable for children and sales to children are illegal. There is clear medical evidence of a strong link between excessive drinking and premature death. In recent years we have all become familiar with the message that drinking and driving can produce a lethal cocktail: for the driver, passengers or innocent victims of accidents. The paradox inherent in these views was recently highlighted in December 1995 when the British Government revised upwards recommended safe drinking levels for men and women, within days of a new campaign against drinking before driving. The first measure appeared to encourage people to drink more, the second urged greater restriction.

To some extent the paradox involved in these conflicting attitudes and beliefs resides in the difference between occasional or moderate drinking and regular heavy drinking. The former is regarded as a valuable social lubricant, the latter as a threat to individuals and society.

Even so there is much blurring. In some contexts drunkenness may be viewed as justified by the occasion, 'a laugh' or a 'rite of passage', whilst in other contexts drunks are pitied or scorned. As with violence and aggression, opinion is divided on whether there is a causal link between moderate and excessive drinking. Does the widespread acceptance and indeed promotion of drinking increase the likelihood of large numbers of people becoming addicted? Or should it be possible for everyone to learn to drink safely, as the majority appear to do? The lesson of American Prohibition in the 1920s seemed to be that putting a legal ban on alcohol consumption created more crime and health problems than it solved. Yet countries and cultures which foster high alcohol consumption also have high levels of alcohol related illnesses and other problems (Velleman, 1992).

Whatever the reader's personal experiences and views, it is evident that alcohol consumption is a major social issue. This book is concerned with one particular aspect - the effects on children. The link between alcohol and children takes two main forms. Firstly, many adults are concerned about children themselves drinking too soon and/or too much. A major focus of health education programmes, alongside sex education, HIV/AIDS and drugs, has been to prevent young people acquiring the habit of heavy drinking. Secondly, children may be affected by the drinking patterns of adults in their lives. The effects will be more far-reaching when those adults are the child's parents or someone responsible for their everyday care. It is this second issue which we shall be considering.

A study of parental heavy drinking and its effects on children

At the heart of the book are accounts provided by children and their parents about what it means to grow up in a family where one or both parents has a drink problem. This forms part of a growing trend in the social sciences and in social policy studies to give prominence to children's own perspectives on issues which affect them. The families' experiences were tapped in research carried out by the authors and commissioned jointly by the Health Education Board for Scotland and Barnardos Scotland, following a literature review they had funded which revealed the need for a study of this nature (Shucksmith, 1994).

Concern about the potentially disruptive and violent implications for family life had already led to a number of studies on the effects of parental alcohol misuse on children. Understandably, they had mostly adopted a pathological or problem-oriented approach, with the assumption that the effects must be negative, and that children will have difficulty coping. Whilst this is clearly true in some cases, it does not necessarily apply more universally. Moreover, much of the relevant research has been based on external measures of children's performance, clinical generalisations or retrospective accounts by adults. The experiences and perceptions of children themselves were largely absent in the literature.

The present study was intended to help remedy this shortcoming by providing qualitative information on the perspectives of children. It was intended not only to examine distress and trauma, but also to identify positive consequences and coping mechanisms. Acknowledgement was to be given to the wide diversity of circumstances in which heavy drinking impinges on children.

In the rest of this chapter we shall set the scene, first by reviewing existing knowledge about alcohol and children, then describing how this issue fits with wider changes in attitudes towards children and childhood more generally.

The nature and extent of 'problem drinking' in families with dependent children

It is not easy to assess the extent of alcohol misuse in families, for two main reasons. Firstly, information is usually available about individual adults, rather than families. Sometimes a person's parental status may be given, but it may not be known how many children they have or whether they are still living together. This is part of a wider problem in obtaining statistical data which pertains to children (Qvortrup, 1991). Secondly, the process of defining heavy drinking or alcohol misuse is not straightforward. Consumption in the population is spread widely along a continuum and there is no sharp dividing line (Velleman, 1992).

Drawing the boundaries between 'social' or 'acceptable' drinking and heavy or problematic drinking is therefore somewhat arbitrary, but official dividing lines have been devised (Robertson and Heather, 1992). These are adjusted according to gender and size, both of which influence the physiological effects of alcohol. The British Government's recommended *weekly* limits for alcohol consumption were raised in 1995 from 21 units to 28 for men and from 14 units to 21 for women. One unit is equivalent to half a pint of beer, a glass of wine or a measure of spirits.

The reason these limits are provided is that there is a wealth of evidence about the negative health consequences of excessive alcohol consumption. Prolonged excessive intake has major deleterious effects on bodily and mental functions which can lead to premature death. However, heavy drinking need not be prolonged to be dangerous. Intoxication is a prominent factor in driving and fire accidents and violent crime, including homicide (Velleman, 1992; Gulbenkian Foundation Commission, 1995). In contrast there is no evidence for long-term damage when drinking is below Government recommended levels. Indeed claims have been made that moderate drinking may even be beneficial for a person's physical health.

Our knowledge about how many people drink 'excessively' depends in part of course on the definition of excess used. The main sources of information for large populations are surveys which normally rely on what individuals themselves are prepared to say about their drinking patterns, since it would be expensive and impractical to obtain convincing external checks. Such self-reports may not be accurate, since even in a confidential situation people may not be inclined to state their true level of drinking or may simply misjudge how much they drink. Moreover, heavy drinkers are also less likely to be included in surveys. Some are homeless; others will refuse to co-operate or not bother to respond. With these provisos in mind, we can present some general conclusions which make it clear that problem drinking is very widespread both in terms of the proportion of the population affected and in social and geographical distribution. It affects rich and poor, employed and unemployed, males and females, single people, childless people and parents.

Only about one in ten adults do not drink alcohol at all. It appears that slightly more than one quarter of men and one tenth of women drink beyond the recommended maxima (Shucksmith, 1994). About six percent of men and two per cent of women drink unsafe amounts, more than double the prescribed levels. This amounts to perhaps a million individuals in the UK.

It is not known how many heavy drinkers are parents or carers of children. It seems that on average parents drink less than other adults, but this generalisation masks large variations. One survey, found that nearly one third of fathers of pre-school children drank heavily, i.e. over 21 units per week (Goddard, 1991). At all ages fewer mothers drink heavily, but the numbers are nevertheless significant. About one in ten mothers with a youngest child aged 11-15 reported drinking above the recommended amounts (14 units for women). We do not know how many children are affected by the heavy drinking of *both* parents.

Children's knowledge and understanding of alcoholic drinks

The current study was concerned with the impact on children of *adults'* drinking and not children's own involvement with drinking. Nevertheless these two issues are interconnected, especially as there is evidence that offspring of problem drinkers are more likely than others to drink heavily themselves.

Most children become aware of the distinctiveness of alcoholic drinks at an early age and understand them to be reserved for adults (Jahoda and Cramond, 1972). They also connect alcoholic drinks with drunkenness and tend to disapprove of drunken behaviour. The main sources of information appear to be direct witnessing and television. Knowledge tends to be acquired earlier and is more detailed for children in families with an alcohol-dependent parent (Fossey, 1994). Even so, many children do not realise the extent or seriousness of their parents' drinking (Roosa et al., 1993). Attitudes about drinking are usually negative and as they grow older increased proportions of children show disapproval of drunkenness. Children hold gender stereotypes, so that certain kinds of drink are seen as masculine and they feel more reproachful towards drunken women than drunken men (Fossey, 1994).

Children's knowledge and understanding do not develop in isolation. Besides the influence of family, peers and the media, children have been increasingly exposed to official attempts to modify their views through alcohol education programmes. School-based programmes tend to start with children aged 10-11, when it is thought they are becoming both more exposed to the temptations of alcoholic drink and more able to learn and respond to information about risks and dangers. Controlled evaluations of such programmes, some of which are admittedly quite brief, indicate that they may well affect knowledge, but rarely have a significant effect on attitudes and behaviour (Sharp, 1994). Likewise television campaigns appear to have little influence on consumption (Bennett et al., 1990). Critics argue that all too often programmes ignore the 'rewarding' nature of alcohol consumption and the peer norms which sustain it, so are doomed to fail unless they engage on a more equal level with young people rather than seek to influence from a top-down, adult oriented perspective (May, 1991; 1993).

Children's own consumption of alcoholic drinks

The great majority of children have at least sipped an alcoholic drink during the primary years, although for most the first full drink occurs later, usually around 11-13 (Fossey, 1994). Most children are introduced to alcohol by their parents, who also normally see themselves as the primary educators with regard to drinking (Fossey and Miller, personal communication).

Once into adolescence a number of individuals begin to drink alcohol on a substantial scale, usually outside the home, because they feel it helps them to have a good time with friends. By the age of 15 years as many as a third of children report having had an alcoholic drink at least weekly (Central Statistical Office, 1994). More boys than girls take alcoholic drinks at a younger age, but in the mid teens the proportions of males and females who admit to drinking alcohol weekly is quite similar (Woodroffe et al., 1993). It seems that the number of children who have been drunk by the age of 11 has grown in recent years (Simpson et al, 1993).

Several factors have been found to increase the chances of teenage alcohol 'misuse', although much of the research evidence comes from North America (Sharp, 1994):

- parental heavy drinking

- sibling heavy drinking

- friendships with drinkers

- low self-esteem

- well below average school performance

Children brought up in families which are emotionally close and set clear expectations about acceptable behaviour appear to be least likely to take up heavy drinking (Foxcroft and Lowe, 1995).

The direct impact of parental heavy drinking on children

The implications of parental heavy drinking on children constitute the main subject matter of this book. The term 'parents' is taken to include parental figures, including step-parents.

In a small minority of cases, there seems to be a genetic link between drinking patterns in one generation and the next (Velleman, 1992). Children may also be affected by direct transmission of parental alcohol intake when they develop 'foetal alcohol syndrome' (Edelstein, 1995; McNamara, 1995). This is a condition which results when a foetus absorbs alcohol directly from a mother who engages in heavy drinking during pregnancy. The consequences for the child after birth *may* include slow growth, abnormalities of the head and face, learning disorders and developmental delay.

Much more commonly, though, the impact of heavy drinking on children acts through its effects on parental behaviour and competence. Quantitative comparisons of children in 'alcoholic' and 'non-alcoholic' households have shown that the former include higher proportions with behavioural difficulties and educational deficits, although some of these may be temporary phenomena. Self-esteem and confidence are also adversely affected (Nastasi and DeZolt, 1994). However most children with alcoholic parents do reasonably well and some even shine, though little is known about these 'invulnerables' or about the protective factors in their lives or personalities.

It is known that alcohol-related problems figure prominently in cases of child abuse, receptions into care and the loss of parental rights with respect to children (Lambert et al. 1990; Reder et al., 1993; Simpson et al., 1993; Coleman and Cassell, 1995). Periodic excessive drinking seems much more common as a precipitating factor than consistent heavy drinking (Davidson, 1992). Usually drink is not the sole factor but is compounded with relationship and environmental difficulties.

Research on child protection case conferences (interdisciplinary meetings which consider situations where there is concern that a child has been abused within the family context) revealed significant gender differences with respect to the alleged abuser which appeared related to societal expectations. Drinking mothers were most common in neglect cases, whereas men accounted for most drink-related violence towards children (Simpson et al, 1993). Given the greater responsibilities for housework and child care normally assumed by women, it is to be expected that a drinking mother may affect her children's upbringing more than a drinking father. In their sample of young adults, Velleman and Orford (1990) found that those with mothers who had drinking problems scored significantly higher on a scale of negative childhood experiences compared with those with drinking fathers.

Although there is ample statistical evidence of *what* the implications of heavy drinking are for children, there are rather fewer systematic accounts of *how* children are affected by parental drinking and how this varies according to factors like age, household composition, degree of exposure to drink-related behaviour and the quality of relationships with the both the drinking and non-drinking parent. There is a danger of seeing the alcohol misuse as the only or predominant feature of household relationships. Apart from the most extreme cases, there will be times and sides to the parent which are not affected by the drinking, but which form part of the child's whole experience of family life.

Certainly some children experience violence, fear, disruption of family activities, social embarrassment and social isolation (Orford, 1985). Guilt and worry about parents have also been identified. Velleman and Orford (1990) found that the most frequently recalled effects were parental moodiness, unreliability and disruptions to routines or celebrations like Christmas and birthdays. Not surprisingly, therefore, a greater proportion of children and adolescents with alcoholic parents report unhappiness and depression (Johnson and Rolf, 1990).

In contrast to these negative aspects, some clinical writers have identified a number of roles which may be thought to typify the overall responses of other family members, including children, some of which have positive or mixed connotations. They include 'hero', 'victim', scapegoat', 'lost child', 'mascot', 'persecutor', 'rescuer' and 'enabler' (Fanti, 1990). It is also noted that children are not passive, but adopt various coping mechanisms like hiding bottles, avoidance of the parent when drunk and arranging social activities outside the home (Stafford, 1992). For all these reasons, several writers have pointed to the need to be aware that parental alcohol misuse has different effects on children, depending on the circumstances. It is also important to identify protective and supportive factors which enable some children to cope well despite a parent's heavy drinking.

The indirect effects of heavy drinking

There is much evidence that heavy drinking is associated with disharmony between parents (Orford, 1985) and such discord is known to be detrimental to children (Rutter, 1980; Schaffer, 1990). According to Stafford (1992), alcohol plays a part in half of all cases of domestic violence and one third of divorces. Similarly, alcohol consumption is often a factor in separation and divorce. When there are children involved this will often mean that they lose contact with the parent they do not live with.

Heavy drinking also increases the likelihood of absenteeism from work or job loss, which has knock on effects for family income (Velleman, 1993a).

Longer term effects of excessive drinking on children

Some longitudinal and retrospective studies have been carried out which examine the circumstances of adults who were brought up in a household with a heavy drinking parent. These have shown that offspring of people who misuse alcohol continue to experience above average rates of health and social difficulties in adulthood, especially sons of alcoholic fathers (Werner, 1986; McCord, 1990; Greenfield, 1993). In contrast, factors which appear to account for resilience include temperament, self-belief and achievement orientation.

A substantial study by Velleman and Orford (1993a, 1993b) investigated the experiences of 160 men and women aged sixteen to thirty five who had problem drinking parents. They were compared with 80 young adults whose parents had not been heavy drinkers. Nearly all the offspring of heavy drinkers spoke very negatively about their childhood experiences, much more so than the comparison group. Yet the differences in current life patterns, satisfaction and coping measures were minimal. It appeared that for only a minority had the parental drinking had long term negative consequences. Further examination of their data indicated that persistent problems occurred mainly when there had been family conflict as well as heavy drinking. They concluded that the risks from having a heavy drinking parent were more due to disharmony than the direct effects of the alcohol. They observed that, in the absence of parental discord, there might even be gains from the experience. Family support and cohesion was associated with positive outcomes, whether or not one of the parents had a drinking problem (Velleman, 1993a). A different study also suggested that negative consequences are more likely when drinking is combined with verbal criticism and inhibited communication about feelings (Jones and Houts, 1992).

In adulthood, it seems that children's own drinking patterns often model themselves on their parents to a considerable degree, but there is a tendency to revert to the norm, since offspring of both heavy drinkers and abstainers are less inclined to follow the parental pattern (Shucksmith, 1994).

Services for children and families

There are now a wide range of facilities available for adults with drink problems. Specific treatments include drug therapy, cognitive and behavioural techniques, individual counselling and group work (Velleman, 1992; Goodwin, 1994). These are often used in combination. Addiction services have increasingly sought to engage family members, both to enlist their assistance for the identified drinker and to offer them help in their own right. Until recently, however, family programmes have mostly involved only spouses and partners, not children (Orford, 1985). Partners may be offered support separately or together, and very occasionally the whole family may be included in treatment. More general purpose family and social welfare organisations tend to refer any identified alcohol problem to specialists, with the result that alcohol and family issues are largely dealt with independently (Collins, 1990; Alaszewksi and Harrison, 1992)

A leading commentator in the field has bemoaned the lack of provision to help children of heavy drinking parents (Velleman, 1993b). It appears that when agencies do include children in their clientele, their objective is usually to discourage or tackle adolescent drinking rather than deal with the consequences of parental drinking. Even so, a Scottish survey showed that only a minority of alcohol/addiction agencies in Scotland have more than a few cases where the drinker is a young person (Munro et al. 1994).

There are self-help groups available to older teenagers through the organisation Al-Ateen, but groups are not widespread and do not offer a service to younger children (Velleman, 1993b).

Implications for the study described in this book

Shucksmith (1994) identified that nearly all research had been conducted from an adult perspective, either involving retrospective information from adults about their own experiences or else external assessments by experts, usually as part of correlational outcome studies. Apart from clinical evidence, there was also often little differentiation of the nature and context of the 'problem drinking'. There was little attention to the *processes* which might lead to different outcomes, including personal coping mechanisms and social supports. These have been found to be crucial mediators of children's experiences in relation to other family experiences and stressors (Belle, 1989; Cochrane et al., 1990).

Hence HEBS and Barnardos formulated a brief for a 6-month qualitative investigation, which the present study was devised to implement. The main objectives were:

- to explore, from the child's perspective, the meaning and impact of living within a family where alcohol abuse is a problem

- to explore, from the perspective of family members, the meaning and impact on the children of living within a family where alcohol abuse is a problem

- to identify the needs of children who live within a family where alcohol abuse is a problem, both from the perspective of the child and other members of the family

- to ascertain from family members the value of resources and services already provided or available

- to explore the role and impact of community structures in
  (a) reinforcing acceptance/disapproval of problem drinking
  (b) contributing to or ameliorating the impact of alcohol abuse in the family

- to make recommendations for the establishment of development work with children and families

This was an ambitious set of objectives to be achieved in a relatively short time-scale. The next chapter will describe how we set about trying to fulfil these aims and found it necessary to make some modifications to the planned approach. First, though, it is important to pause and consider certain aspects of adult-child relationships more generally. Whilst the study was specifically about alcohol issues in relation to children, both the research and its topic represent an example of how children's lives and adult understandings of their experiences are significantly influenced by adult expectations and presumptions.

Changing views of children and childhood

The last decade has witnessed a significant shift in prevailing ideas about children, both in the legal/policy sphere and in academic discourse. In particular, these confer much greater legitimacy and salience to children's own perspectives than had usually been the case previously. How far the new approaches represent major changes in how children are actually treated remains open to question. Nevertheless they have implications for the way research is conducted and findings interpreted. They also affect, or should affect, the nature of services and policies developed to promote children's interests and development - a point we shall return to in the final chapter.

Children's rights

In recent years, both national and international law have given increased priority to children's rights (Archard, 1993; Asquith and Hill, 1994; Franklin, 1995). The UN Convention on the Rights of the Child was signed in 1989 and subsequently ratified by most governments in the world, including that of the UK in 1991. This set out over 40 different rights for children about which it was possible to achieve broad consensus amongst nearly all nations. Children's rights also figured prominently in the Children Act 1989, which mainly affected England & Wales, and in more recent legislation in Scotland and Northern Ireland (1995). The rights specified in these documents and statutes embody beliefs that children should as far as possible exercise similar rights to any other persons, while recognising that they are also specially vulnerable to exploitation so that additional protection is necessary.

There are many common misconceptions about children's rights. They have sometimes been caricatured as meaning children have the freedom to do just what they want. Instances are cited of children seeking to 'divorce' from their parents or demanding purchases parents cannot afford. In fact, the rights embodied in the UN Convention and specific laws do not give children 'carte blanche', but do entitle them to be consulted and have their views taken account of in any significant decision affecting their lives. This means that adults must take seriously the opinions and wishes of children. The law also recognises that decision-making should make allowances for the age and level of understanding of a child. It is important that this proviso is not misused by adults who may be only too ready to assume that a child is too young to make a contribution or to be affected. With respect to experiences such as divorce, child abuse and adoption, it has been shown that children are more deeply affected than many adults think and that, given the right information and means of communication, they can convey their thoughts and feelings from an early age (Mitchell, 1985; Brodzinsky et al., 1984; Spencer and Flin, 1991). This highlights the importance of obtaining the perspectives of even young children on alcohol and its effects.

The right of children to express their views is just one type of right. There are two other major categories of right contained in the UN Convention - to protection and provision. The Convention recognises parental rights and duties to bring up children as they consider appropriate, but also points to limits on family and parental autonomy. If children are subject to ill-treatment or neglect within the family, they are entitled to outside protection. This may take the form of State intervention, including where necessary protecting children by separation from their family environment (Hammarberg, 1994). The British state has had powers to intervene in situations of 'cruelty' and abuse from the time of the Poor Law, but it remains a matter of contention when and how to do so without causing more harm than good (Parton, 1991; Hendrick, 1993). Nevertheless, it is clear that if adults' drinking has adverse effects on their children outside action may be justified in the interests of the child.

Children's rights to provision represent a more positive role for public agencies. Governments are obliged by the UN Convention to make available facilities which support families when this is needed to protect children or further their welfare. Recent British legislation too requires local authorities to provide services for 'children in need' (Hill and Aldgate, 1996). This category, superficially broad, has been criticised for focusing narrowly on children at risk. Nevertheless, it includes children whose health or development would otherwise be impaired and so is clearly relevant to children adversely affected by parental alcohol misuse.

Child-centred approaches in social science

Parallel developments have occurred in the academic world which accord greater importance than previously to children's perspectives. Interest in children's own views and in the social processes which shape adult percpetions of childhood have become much more central within the social sciences. There has of course been a long tradition of studying children which has produced a wealth of information and concepts about children. This has mostly come from developmental and experimental approaches in child psychology, although also from more applied subjects like medicine, education and social work. Sociology and anthropology, disciplines which focus more on the social than the individual, have for the most part given little attention to children except when they have become old enough to become part of youth studies.

The body of conventional theorising on children built up over decades has been criticised on three main grounds. First, the aim has been to acquire seemingly objective knowledge about the general nature of childhood, whereas critics suggest that childhood is 'socially constructed' (Rogers 1992; Qvortrup et al. 1994). In other words, the main features of children's lives are not predetermined by biological inheritance and maturation but develop through social interaction, which varies greatly according to time, culture and place. Moreover children themselves contribute to establishing the meanings and structures of their experiences, both individually and collectively (James and Prout, 1990). This alternative viewpoint is aligned with more general interpretive traditions within social science which stress the importance of the subjective meaning of experience as opposed to the abstraction and quantification of social 'facts'.

Secondly, it is argued that children have been treated mainly as objects of study. This is seen in most extreme form in the application of experimental approaches or the use of standard external measures and questionnaires, when children feature purely as reactors and respondents to predetermined stimuli and questions. It also means that the types of topic chosen and methods used reflect adults' rather than children's concerns, so that even when children have been asked their views the prompts have been standardised in advance.

Thirdly, it has been suggested that the prevailing developmental perspective on children has exaggerated the differences between adults and children. In particular, it has portrayed children as lacking adult competencies and has undervalued the knowledge and skills they possess (Mayall, 1994; Ennew, 1994). The popular framework developed by Piaget has come in for particular criticism for underestimating children's capacities. This links with the point made above about adults in general devaluing children.

Some of these points may be exaggerated and over generalised. For some time now, developmental psychologists have abandoned the earlier passive view of children as empty recepticles of socialisation processes (LaFontaine, 1986). They now emphasise the active role of children in shaping their own lives (Richards and Light, 1986; Woodhead et al., 1991). Moreover, it has been recognised that children's understanding can be underestimated because adults have not communicated with them in ways which enable them to express themselves effectively (Donaldson, 1978; Cox, 1980). Open-ended research has taken place in the past which seeks to comprehend how children see the world (e.g. Furth, 1980). Even so, it is true that there has been a dearth of studies which start from children's point of view and engage them in determining what the salient issues are.

What some have called a new paradigm has emerged in reaction to the deficiencies of earlier approaches (James and Prout, 1990). Initially this was mainly concerned with examining and questioning adult views, writings and statistics about childhood and children. Increasingly, though, portraits have been made of aspects of children's lives which draw on children's own perspectives - for instance in relation to television (Buckingham, 1993), health (Mayall, 1993) and the use of time and space (Solberg, 1990; Ennew, 1994).

Children and research

In the light of these observations, it is beholden to adult researchers dealing with children to optimise the opportunities for children to convey their points of view. This is best suited to qualitative research, in which open-ended techniques are used to explore issues in depth, with participants helping to define the agenda. It is rare, though, for researchers to have a free hand and usually compromises are necessary which take account of specifications from funders or stakeholders in the research.

Ethnographic studies in which researchers spend time alongside children are often particularly effective in gaining trust and eliciting confidences (e.g. Bluebond-Langner, 1978; James, 1993). However, some experiences occur privately and/or unexpectedly, including exposure to drunken behaviour. Others are prolonged and cumulative, so less amenable to outside observation, as in the case of long-term alcohol misuse. In such cases, it is necessary to obtain verbal reports after the event through interviews.

Research with children should strike a balance between recognising their competence and status as informants, whilst recognising the implications of differences in experience and power (Bury, 1993; Barbour and Brown, 1995). The influences which affect interviews with adults are also relevant to children, such as the need to establish rapport, ensure confidentiality or pose questions clearly and concisely, but there are also additional factors. Communication with children needs to be adapted to their level of cognitive and linguistic development; to make use of materials, techniques and settings with which they are familiar; and to convey instructions in a manner which makes sense from a child's perspective (Garbarino et al., 1992). Hence the interviewer's skills, manner and ability to see things from each child's point of view are crucial. It is important to be aware of extensive evidence that children in interview situations are strongly affected by the perceived power and status of adults and by presumptions about what answers are expected

Non-verbal aids to communication with children have been widely used in therapeutic, educational and recreational contexts (Astrop, 1982; Redgrave, 1987; Ryan and Walker, 1993). Some of these can be adapted for research purposes, such as use of diagrams and play materials; word-choice and sentence completion exercises; vignettes and trigger stories (Hill and Triseliotis, 1990). Game-like tasks and photos were employed by Jahoda and Cramond (1972) and replicated by Fossey (1994) to assess primary school children's knowledge and attitudes concerning alcohol.

Ideally, children - like any research participants - should be given full information about what the research entails and an opportunity to reflect before committing themselves to take part (Alderson, 1995). They should also have the choice to discontinue involvement at any time (Rheingold, 1982). It is normally necessary also to obtain the agreement of parents or guardians who have legal responsibilities for children and of 'gatekeepers' (e.g. schools) who may provide access to children. In the study described in this book, we had to rely on the adults to communicate with the children on our behalf beforehand, but sought as far as possible to give children choices about the conduct of the interviews and respected their wishes when they made it clear they preferred not to discuss a particular topic.

Summary

This book represents part of a growing trend to give a voice to children. Much has been written about adults' alcohol misuse, including the effects on children of parental heavy drinking. However, direct accounts by children or indeed their parents are rarely included. It is their experiences, often reported in their own words, which are central in the chapters which follow.

In our society, alcoholic drinks are widely consumed, socially acceptable and indeed thought desirable in many contexts. Yet, taken in excess, they also lead to damage and even death to the drinker and others. Although precise details are hard to establish, there is much evidence that many parents drink to excess. It has also been established that the offspring of parents who misuse alcohol have significantly more problems than the general population. On the other hand, many are apparently resilient and do well in adulthood. Second-hand or retrospective accounts are available which depict what it is like to grow up with a heavy drinking parent, but the voice of children themselves has seldom been heard on this topic.

Therefore a study was commissioned by the Health Education Board for Scotland and Barnardos Scotland which would remedy this situation by talking with children and their parents to ascertain the impact of alcohol misuse on the children. This approach is in tune with other developments in policy, theory and research which highlights the importance of learning from children directly how they experience and interpret their social worlds.

2 Research design, methodological issues and fieldwork

Social researchers expend much time and effort on the design of their studies. Also reports of research often give the impression of a neat and tidy connection between the original plan and actual execution. Artificial experiments and highly standardised surveys may approach this ideal, but in doing so often leave out the complexities of reality as it is actually experienced day by day. By contrast qualitative research aims to capture the meanings and significance of everyday life, so that it is less able to impose controls and boundaries on the samples and subject matter, but must adjust to people's willingness and ability to provide relevant data. This is particularly true for studies of sensitive topics like ours which usually entail a considerable degree of shame and secrecy (Renzetti and Raymond, 1995)

Consequently, the design of qualitative research may well be modified as it proceeds. That was very much the case with the present study. We knew at the outset that parents would not be queuing up to have us learn about the details of their 'alcohol problems', let alone allow us to speak with their children who might well make embarrassing or critical revelations. Ingenuity and careful reassurances would be needed to reach and engage with families willing to take part in the study. We began with specific ideas about the type of sample we hoped to achieve and the kinds of interviews we wished to carry out, but were also prepared to amend our plans as the fieldwork evolved. In this chapter we detail our sometimes circuitous and even painful progress from initial design to eventual outcome.

The difficulties we encountered and the adaptations we had to make are relevant to interpretation of the findings of the study, but perhaps just as important also reflect some of the difficulties and selectivity likely to affect attempts to set up services for children of drinking parents. Although there are significant differences between asking for information (to help others) and offering a service, lessons can be drawn from the similar processes involved in identifying and engaging potential recruits.

Initial design

The outline, scope and time scale of the study was predetermined in our remit from the funders, though the methodological details were elaborated by us. We were to carry out an intensive, qualitative survey of up to 20 families in which one or both parents had an identified drinking problem. The focus of the survey was to be on the children's experience of living with parental heavy drinking, as revealed both in their own first-hand accounts and in the second-hand accounts of their parents. The research was to last 6 months from the preparatory stage to submission of the final report.

Sampling

A two-tiered sample was planned as follows:

1. The main sample would be of families who had at least one compulsory school-age child (5-16), and at least one parent or parent figure with a drinking problem. As far as possible, the children would be still be living with the drinking parents or have been separated from them only recently, so that they could provide fresh commentaries on the drinking situation. Both the children and the parents were to be interviewed.

2. A subsidiary sample would consist of young adults (from 18-22) who had grown up in a family with at least one parent or parent figure with a drinking problem. They would be asked to give retrospective accounts which would be influenced by their later experiences and reflections.

It was neither appropriate nor practical to obtain a strictly representative sample for this study. Instead, the intention was to obtain a purposive layered sample which covered a wide range of relevant family settings. It was hoped to include a fairly even spread of ages and gender in the sample, with lone parent and reconstituted households as well as those that were intact. Efforts would also be made to achieve a reasonable mix of social backgrounds. For convenience and economy, the sample was to be recruited mainly from the Glasgow area, but a few families living in rural districts were to be included too.

It was anticipated that the best way to gain access to appropriate families within a reasonable time scale would be through formal agencies. The use of direct appeals to the public through advertising was thought unlikely to produce a major response and even then anyone who came forward in that way could well be atypical, perhaps with an axe to grind. A long-term ethnographic approach in one or two particular neighbourhoods might well have been successful, but required more resources than were available to us.

In order to improve the chances of obtaining a wide cross-section of families, it was planned to make contacts through a range of voluntary and statutory bodies, as well as self-help groups. They included health and social services, specialist alcohol agencies, multi-purpose organisations and family support groups.

Interviewing

For the main sample, it was considered important to hold separate interviews with the children and with their parent or parents. This would minimise the possibility of influence or even intimidation, and ensure that the individuals concerned could feel free to give their own perspective on the situation in privacy and without fear of repercussions. Where two parents were living in the household, they would be interviewed separately, for similar reasons. Parents would be interviewed on only one occasion each. However, we thought it would be desirable to see children on more than one occasion, in order to build up a relationship of trust. Time would not permit such intensive contacts with every child in every family, so it was proposed that in multi-child households, one child be selected as the 'focus child' for intensive interviewing, and supplementary pair or group discussions be held with the child's siblings.

In the subsidiary sample, the young adults would be interviewed on their own on one occasion only. Their parents would not be interviewed, nor would we meet their siblings.

Interviews with children, parents and young adults were planned as semi-structured, with a number of standard themes to be covered. These included:

- The child's perceptions of drinking

- Family and parent-child communication about drinking

- The child's relationship with the adult(s) who has (have) a drink problem

- The child's activities and family routines

- Impact of drink related behaviour on the child

- The child's and family's coping capacities and mechanisms

- The role of other non-drinking family members

- The role of social networks and formal agencies

- Ideas for support services

The style and content of each interview would depend on who was being interviewed. Parents would give their accounts of their children's responses to the drinking, whereas young adults would provide retrospective reports of their childhood experiences. With both, the interviewer would aim to cover each major theme in a flexible and sensitive manner to enable he interviewee to describe their own experiences and views in their own words. Whereas standardised questions yield specific answers on matters foreseen by the researchers, this approach encourages the emergence and identification of new issues and perspectives.

The nature and style of the interviews with children were to vary according to their age, level of understanding and willingness to settle or concentrate. Here it was important to supplement verbal questioning with the use of pictures and exercises (e.g. word-choice charts). This would help motivation and concentration by making the interviews more interesting. At the same time it would allow scope for children to express themselves in different ways, given the barriers which can sometimes arise as a result of differences in power and communication modes between adults and children. The overriding consideration was to conduct the interviews with children in a flexible manner to optimise communication (Garbarino et al., 1992; Hill et al., 1996).

As is usual, children, parents and young adults were all to be offered guarantees of confidentiality and anonymity, and assured that their identity would in no circumstances be revealed in any publication or discussion outside the research team. In view of the research remit to concentrate on family perspectives and the short time scale, no information about individual cases was to be gathered from professionals or case records.

The research in practice

The original intention was to complete the main interviewing stage within three months, halfway through the project, leaving ample time for unhurried analysis and writing up. In fact by that point we had only met one family, with offers of meetings from three more. Qualitative interview studies do not necessarily require large samples, but a sample of four would clearly stretch credibility. Our difficulties and the reasons for them were not unexpected. First we outline the problems in gaining access, then describe how the situation was retrieved.

Access

It was clear even in the planning stages of the project that the main problem would lie in gaining access to cases, especially as there were only a few weeks in which to conduct multiple negotiations. Problem drinking is notoriously a taboo subject and the literature is replete with references to denial, secrecy, guilt and shame, not only on the part of drinkers, but also of their families. Even drinkers who are prepared to admit to outsiders that they have a problem often deny that it affects their children. To compound that difficulty, we were expecting drinkers not only to talk to us themselves about these highly charged and sensitive issues, but to allow their children to speak to us about them. In effect, we were asking parents to let their children talk to us about intimate parental problems.

Even so, we knew from previous experience that some individuals are prepared to take part in research on sensitive issues, provided this is seen as in a good cause and is sensitively handled with appropriate guarantees of confidentiality and anonymity. We therefore considered the research was feasible, if 'challenging'. It would however require intensive networking of local organisations.

Preliminary discussions with professionals in the field suggested that we might realistically achieve an average of 2-3 cases from each source approached. A start was therefore made by drawing up a list of ten mainstream agencies, including Social Work Department area teams and addiction units, Health Board hospitals and voluntary sector alcohol services. A private hospital was also included in the hope of reaching families who have few contacts with mainstream public services. All these agencies were approached at management level to seek formal approval for collaboration. Some managers were enthusiastic about the prospects of families participating in the study, whilst others spoke cautiously of probable defensiveness or unpredictability. However, nearly all recognised the importance of the research and agreed to assist by asking fieldworkers to approach families on our behalf. To widen the access net and reach families who might not be in touch with agencies, a limited advertising drive for volunteers was also undertaken through posters in health centres, libraries and student unions.

In the event, access to cases proved a much slower process than hoped for, due to a number of factors:

- Managers and fieldworkers were often rightly concerned about the sensitivity of the topic. Time was spent with them, to explain the rationale for the study, give reassurances about confidentiality and anonymity, and suggest how they might go about approaching families.

- Even workers who were eager to help experienced considerable difficulty in persuading individuals and families to meet us. Typically, they would identify three or four 'probable' families, only to find that most or even all declined to take part. The refusal was often on the part of the parent, but sometimes when parents wished to take part the children themselves refused. Young adults also proved hard to persuade. A few workers made heroic efforts to recruit families on our behalf, without success.

- Even when workers were eventually able to find us cases, this took some time. Some were not in close touch with the drinkers, so special efforts had to be made to seek them out. Alternatively a drinker who had regular appointments would suddenly go on a 'binge' and disappear from the professional's view for a time.

- One way of augmenting numbers in qualitative research is 'snowballing', i.e. asking individuals already contacted to suggest other possible cases from their acquaintance. Despite the willingness of most families to help, those who tried to snowball for us faced the same difficulty as fieldworkers; they could think of families they were sure would take part, but were unable to persuade them to do so. In fact the only family recruited through another were actually in the sample family's house at the time of interview, so we were able to approach them directly.

- The advertising drive produced no response at all. This was also the experience of researchers in the 'Children Who Care' study on which our project remit had been partly based (Aldridge & Becker, 1994). With sensitive topics such as these, it seems that a personal approach may be essential.

All this meant that by the halfway point the research had fallen well behind schedule. Nevertheless, we were reasonably confident that the seeds planted in our extensive network of contacts would eventually bear fruit, given a little more time. We therefore sought and were granted an extension to the project by two months. In addition we widened further our range of contacts to include less obvious sources, including direct and indirect personal connections, both professional and social.

These steps turned out to be effective, as one by one the cases trickled in. Five and a half months after the start of the study, the twentieth family agreed to take part. Three others had also initially agreed, but changed their minds. To achieve this number of cases, we had negotiated with over 40 agencies, projects or individuals, which represented more than two for every family who eventually took part.

Table 2.1 gives details of the sources from which cases were successfully recruited.

Table 2.1
Sources for the sample

Agency type	Number of offices	Number of cases
Voluntary Alcohol Agencies	7	8
SWD Addiction Units	2	3
Health Centres	2	2
Hospital Addiction Units	2	1
Family and Child agencies	1	1
Health Board Community Addiction Unit	1	1
Educational Psychologist	1	1
Church Minister	1	1
Personal contact of colleague	1	1
Personal contact of research family	1	1
TOTAL	19	21

Characteristics of the sample

As our sample was opportunistic, there are likely to be biases as regards their social characteristics, but the nature of these remain unknown. The features of the total population of children in families with alcohol problems is unclear, even for a limited geographical area or for particular agencies, so we have no way of knowing how typical our sample may be. On the other hand we tried hard to ensure that routes into the sample were diverse enough to give a reasonable mix.

The difficulty in recruiting cases had a knock on effect on the composition of our sample. We had envisaged a sample of 20 cases split between families with children aged 5-16, and independent young adults aged 18-22. In fact, cases were so precious that we were in no position to insist on these limits. In the event, we met 27 children and young adults ranging in age from 5 to 28 years, all of whom had spent at least part of their childhood with at least one drinking parent.

In the sample as in life there was no neat dividing line between 'children' and 'young adults'. In presenting the findings, a division at age 17 will be used. This distinguished the individuals who had left schools from those still at school. On this basis, the age distribution of the sample was categorised as follows:

Primary school children - aged 5-11 years   8

Secondary school children - aged 11-16 years   10
Young adults - aged 17-28 years   9

At times we shall also distinguish the youngest children by referring to them as 'young Primary'.

In some cases we only met one child from the family, but in a few instances we met with two or three sisters and brothers, so that the interviews concerned 20 family situations of problem parental drinking. Just two children in the sample were only children, but in most multi-child families only one or some of the brothers and sisters were seen, for various reasons. In all, six sets of siblings took part in the research. There were five pairs of school-aged children and a threesome consisting of a primary school child and two young adults.

Table 2.2 shows the eventual sample characteristics as regards family size, age and gender. These achieved a spread for family size and age of children in accordance with the original targets, but there was a higher proportion of females than anticipated:

Table 2.2
Characteristics of the sample
(Children and young adults)

A. FAMILY SIZE (N=20)

Only children	2
Two child families	7
Larger families (3+ children)	11

B. AGE (N=27)

5-11	8
12-16	10
Young adults	9

C. GENDER (N=27)

Female	16
Male	11

D. GENDER & AGE (N=27)

	Females	Males
5-11	4	4
12-16	9	3
Young adults	3	4

There were more females than males in the overall sample, even though two of the young adults were necessarily male since they were recruited through a project in a men's prison. In the Secondary group, girls outnumbered boys by 3:1. While in a sample this size that result could well arise by chance, we think it may be significant. Some workers reported a greater reluctance on the part of teenage boys to meet us. A group worker said that in her experience boys and girls are equally forthcoming about parental drinking problems at primary school age, but in adolescence boys are notably more reticent than girls. Velleman and Orford (1993b) found in their retrospective study of children of problem drinkers, that men were more difficult to recruit than women. This could have implications for service provision, which might encounter a similar differential unless carefully designed.

Lone parent households were also over-represented in the sample (Table 2.3):

Table 2.3
Household types

'Intact'	9
Lone parent	9
Reconstituted	2
TOTAL	20

Our aim was to include families with mothers and families with fathers as the identified drinker (ID). It was not always easy to determine this. There was an inherent difficulty since it is a matter of interpretation whether the amount or nature of drinking constitutes a 'problem'. There was agreement amongst children, parents and referral person for the majority of families, but we did not always have a prior indication from an agency about who was the ID. Also, more than once we were told that one parent was the drinker, only to find in the interviews statements or indications that both parents misused alcohol. Occasionally there was inconsistency between what children and parents said. A few of the youngest did not differentiate between their parents' drinking levels though the parents themselves made a distinction.

We have therefore relied either on young adult or parental accounts to define the problem drinkers, since they seemed to be based on the most extensive experience. This yielded a higher number of IDs than either the children's or the referring agencies' accounts. On that basis, in about a third of the households both parents were identified drinkers (Table 2.4):

Table 2.4
Gender of the identified problem drinker
(includes non-biological parents)

Father only	9
Mother only	4
Father and Mother*	7

* includes some parents of children in lone-parent households at the time of interview

It had been expected that more of the problem drinking parents would be male, which turned out to be the case. However, we were successful in recruiting a number of mothers who were the sole ID as well as a sizeable proportion of cases in which both parents were problem drinkers. In eight of the lone parent households, the lone parent was the identified drinker.

The original intention had been to talk with children whose parents were still drinking heavily or had done so recently. They would give a current account of life with a drinking parent, whilst the young adult subsample would give retrospective accounts of what this had been like in the past. Again these distinctions were blurred in the eventual sample. Some of the younger adults were still living with their drinking parents, whose behaviour continued to impinge on them, so they were able to give us current accounts. Some children (even the youngest ones) were no longer exposed to parental drinking, either because of a separation, or because the parent was now recovered. Thus they gave us retrospective information.

Since drinking problems arise at all levels of society, our hope had been to recruit cases from a range of social backgrounds. We had been warned that middle class families might be harder to recruit. In fact we achieved a fairly wide social spread as regards occupation and housing type. Although we did not enquire about income, many of the children and young adults had been raised in (or on the margins of) poverty, since most of the families were reliant on state benefits. In only a minority of households in the sample was there a parent engaged in paid employment. However, in three of these households the parents were professionals.

Thus in terms of these straightforward individual and social characteristics, the sample largely reached its targets and did represent a fair social mix. It is inevitably the case with small qualitative studies that it is hard to know how typical the sample was (Bulmer, 1986). However, we think there are types of family and drinking situation which were absent or underrepresented.

The recruitment process specifically excluded some categories of family. We did not seek to include families with pre-school children.

The Social Work Department requested that no child currently in residential or foster care be included, though we did meet one family where that had happened in the past. At the other end of the spectrum, since we recruited families almost entirely through outside agencies and groups, we did not meet any who had only mild drinking problems.

We only made contact with families when parents were in agreement (apart from the young adult subsample). As a result we mainly met families where parents admitted that they had a problem and who accepted this affected the children. Virtually by definition, families who are reluctant to talk with outsiders would not participate in our study.

Although family circumstances were quite diverse, the sample was fairly homogeneous in certain other respects. All had experienced fairly severe, long-standing drinking problems sufficient in seriousness to bring them into contact with an outside agency. In most cases the parent had been able to form positive, trusting relationships with at least one key worker. Finally, as already mentioned, participation in the study was quite often at least partly motivated by the altruistic desire to help others. Here are examples from three different families:

> *Mother* - Well, if it goes on to help somebody else, I think that's the great thing.
> *Father* (ID) adds - "I felt really good about it when Ricky [the family's worker] asked me, because I thought there's nothing for the children - nothing at all, so any contribution you can make is a help."
>
> *Father* (ID) - David [his worker] says to me, you're under no obligation but I heard it was Barnardo's an' its the kids. I been there, I know what it's like.
>
> *Mother*, partner of (ID) - It's good to feel that out of all the time we've had, something good can come. That's why the girls agreed to talk - they said to help other children. That's the whole reason.

Overall, then, the pattern of the children's sample was one of heavy drinking with serious though not the most extreme consequences, probably combined with a greater than average preparedness to respond positively and openly. To some extent the interviews with young adults provided a corrective, as their experiences usually entailed more severe parental drink problems and greater denial of the issue by their parents. The majority had experienced major disruptions in their lives because of parental drinking, yet recalled little help being sought or given to their families. For instance, three of the young adults had been placed in residential schools on account of their delinquent behaviour. One young adult described his parents' unwillingness to admit they had difficulties and their hostility towards official agencies and professionals. Another said there had been no outside intervention, as far as he was aware. Furthermore, whilst our family interviews often suggested a warm relationship existed between the child and at least one parent, most of the young adults conveyed a bleaker story. Several had experienced drunken violence, and seven of the nine had little or nothing good to say about their parents. It may be that the children's sample gives an unduly positive view (though it certainly revealed children facing many major difficulties and worries), whereas the young adults were mostly sited at an opposite extreme. This should not be taken to imply that family experiences will get worse as children become young adults. Rather it reflects the different ways we obtained the two subsamples. For example, two of the young adults were located via a prison addiction project.

Although the prime purpose of the study was to tap directly the perspectives of children and their parents, we additionally carried out systematic interviews with a number of professionals working with families or children where alcohol was an issue. This enabled us to obtain information and impressions from them about a wider range of children of drinking parents. Their views are presented in Chapter 9 and enabled us to contextualise the findings from the families. We also met with a group of four Secondary children who were attending a specialist unit for children of adult drinkers. We make occasional reference to their views in later chapters.

The interview processes

Just as our plans for recruitment had to be modified in the light of experience, so did our plans for the interviews.

Interviews with the children As intended we were able in every case to interview children separately from their parents. The two interviewers went together by appointment to the family home and met first with the parent/s to explain the research, answer questions and obtain signed consent to proceed. The interviewers then separated off to different rooms to conduct parallel interviews with children and parents. This arrangement worked well. The fact that another interviewer was seeing their parent(s) at the same time seemed to communicate tacitly to children that they had permission to speak openly. Several made reference to this in a way which suggested they found it reassuring.

However, our plans for a systematic combination of individual and sibling interviews were soon modified. Both parents and children had very definite ideas about which children we were to see and how. It was important to respond to their expressed preferences. In some cases, there was only one child of a suitable age; in others, parents only wished us to see one of their children, whilst sometimes only one child in a family had agreed to meet us. As a result, there turned out to be only six families in which more than one child agreed to see us. Of these, one sibling pair were seen apart as they seemed reluctant to settle when together. Four pairs wished to be interviewed jointly not individually. In the other family the school age child was interviewed alone and two young adult siblings were seen together. Therefore, as far as the children's sample was concerned, we ended up with either individual interviews or sibling interviews, but not both as originally proposed.

The plan to see every child on at least two occasions was also abandoned at an early stage. This was tried at first but on two occasions children expressed tension or uncertainty about the nature of the second contact. By contrast, single interviews seemed more comfortable for the children, forming a completed experience which appeared to leave them with a sense of accomplishment. In any case, rapport was quickly established with the children, so it seemed possible to build up sufficient trust on one occasion to cover the required topics. Therefore that became the pattern for the remainder of the sample.

The precise location of the interviews was decided in response to family preferences. The majority took place in the child's bedroom. In one household the child and young adult interviews were carried out simultaneously in the living room.

For the interviews with younger children and those in their early teens, a special format was developed, which included several non-verbal prompts and exercises to stimulate interest and facilitate communication (See Appendix 1). The interviews followed a broad standard sequence, but with open-ended questions and prompts adapted to the situation:

- an ice-breaking discussion of the child's interests, and relationships

- understanding of alcohol

- the salience and implications of alcohol consumption within the family.

- service provision.

To develop rapport, the interviews began with a worksheet entitled 'My likes and dislikes'. During this exercise many children spontaneously referred to people and events relevant to the subsequent discussion of alcohol. This topic was then addressed non-threateningly by means of a card game. Children were shown a pack of 6 cards with pictures on one side of a range of drinks, both alcoholic (beer, wine, vodka, whisky) and non-alcoholic (Coke and Tango). On the backs of the cards were cartoon characters which younger children enjoyed identifying (e.g. 'That's Daffy Duck!'). The cards were placed face down, then the children turned them over one at a time, as in Patience. They were questioned about which ones they liked, had tasted, were allowed to drink and so on. In this way the interviewer was able to gauge the child's awareness of drink and drunkenness in order to contextualise their subsequent account of parental drinking.

The next stage was to ask children about who in their own family drank alcohol. All responded to this, apart from one child aged 10 whose clear reluctance to tackle this was respected:

Interviewer - Does your Mum drink any of them?
Child - Nope (in definite tone)
Interviewer - You don't want to talk about it, do you?
Child shakes head
Interviewer - No? That's OK...that's fine.

Written and visual prompts were shown to help the children express themselves about their responses to their parents when drunk. For instance, they chose words which corresponded with drunken behaviour and their associated emotions (e.g. happy, angry, excited). This led on to further questions about the impact of drink-related behaviour on them. Finally, children were invited to comment on desirable features of service provision and encouraged to discuss their wishes and expectations for the future.

For older adolescents the same semi-structured interview schedule was used as with the young adults (see below), with allowances for the difference in age and perspective.

Interviews with young adults The interviews with young adults went pretty much according to plan. Each was interviewed on a single occasion for about an hour. The locations for the interviews were negotiated individually and so varied according to convenience and choice. Four were held at home, two in the researcher's office, two in prison and one at a social work office.

We had not set out to interview the parents of young adults, but in three instances did so for different reasons. In two cases workers had already arranged for us to meet the parents before we realised that the 'children' we intended to speak to were over 16. In another case, two adult sisters happened to be at home when we called to see a younger child and we took the opportunity to interview them while waiting for their father to return home. Thus, matching interviews with parents occurred with respect to four of the young adults.

A more comprehensive schedule was used for the young adults than for the children (See Appendix 2). They were, of course, asked to reflect on a longer period of time, and it was also possible to include more abstract and general questions. Besides covering recollections of parental drinking, and how it was perceived and responded to at the time, the young adults were also asked to assess the long-term impact and its current salience in their lives.

The parent interviews The majority of parent interviews were completed on one occasion, as planned. However, the interviews were often very long. The intention had been to keep accounts of the drinking history to the minimum needed to understand its impact on the child. In practice, despite the best efforts of the interviewer, the interview often centred on this for a considerable time. Many parents (both IDs and their partners) seemed understandably preoccupied with their own experience of living and coping with problem drinking. They seemed to need to talk at length about their own feelings before they were able to move on to looking at their children's needs, about which many also had much to say. On two occasions a second interview was needed.

Our intention had been to see separately both parents of the children in every two-parent household, but this again proved impracticable. Only four families had both parents at home. In two cases they were interviewed separately as planned. In a third case the couple clearly wished to be seen together, and in the fourth case, picked up as the project was nearing completion, time constraints made it difficult to arrange a meeting with the second parent.

The parent interview outline (see Appendix 3) was loosely structured around a series of themes, using a 'funnelling' technique as suggested by Gelles (1987) for dealing with highly sensitive topics. The interview started with emotionally neutral and positive areas (background information about child and family) progressing towards more difficult areas (drinking history, impact on child and family) and ending on a more positive note with a discussion of possible supports and services.

The parents usually spoke with great openness and most showed considerable insight and painful awareness of the effect drinking had had on their children. This probably reflects the fact that they were a self selected group who had reached us precisely because of their ability to relate warmly and talk freely to outsiders. They had thought deeply about their situations, and had come to the interview prepared to tell us their story. Many had done so specifically in the hope that in doing so they would help other children of drinking parents.

Recording and analysis

The interviews with parents, children and young adults were recorded on audio-tape, with one exception when a 15 year old refused. Each tape was listened to carefully. Key sections were transcribed, particularly from the children's interviews, and the rest of each interview summarised using a set of headings developed by the research team. As with most qualitative research (Walker, 1985; Silverman, 1993), there had been ongoing reflection on the data throughout the fieldwork. To focus conclusions from that process, brainstorming sessions were held in order to pool, group and record important themes. The researchers reviewed each other's written material to act as a check on overly subjective interpretations and to offer further insights. In order to reduce the risk of selecting examples to fit preconceptions, efforts were also made to locate counter-examples or 'negative' cases (Becker, 1961). Although the analysis was primarily qualitative, it was possible to quantify certain data derived from standard questions (e.g. about children's expressed wishes for their parent to stop drinking, how they felt when the parent was drink and how they accounted for the parent's drinking behaviour).

Methodological and ethical issues arising from the fieldwork

A number of interesting issues arose in the course of the fieldwork, which may well have relevance to other parent-child studies, and to service provision for children of adult drinkers.

Confidentiality

There are two distinct aspects to confidentiality in a study such as this. First, can and should participants be assured that they will not be indentified or identifiable in any verbal or written reporting which arises from the research? Second, what position is taken as regards secrecy about information obtained from people in the same family household?

Our intention had been to give global assurances to families of confidentiality and anonymity under all circumstances. However, as we soon discovered, a precondition of co-operation from some agencies is that there be limits to confidentiality. Specifically, we were asked by the Social Work Department for assurances that if in the course of our contact with a family we discovered evidence of possible abuse or neglect we would disclose it to them. Furthermore, a medical ethics committee required that parents should be informed in advance of such potential 'breaches' of confidentiality.

This presented us with a dilemma. Telling parents about the proviso might arouse fears and make them reluctant to take part in the study. On the other hand, not telling them about it would run contrary to the notion of informed consent, to which we were committed. We decided to be open with parents about the circumstances in which we would feel obliged to breach the confidentiality of which we were otherwise assuring them. This was carefully presented, in general terms which made the exceptional nature of the proviso clear: 'For example, if we went into a family and discovered that someone's life was in danger, or a child was at serious risk'. This not only seemed acceptable to the families we met, but was explicitly approved by some. No family withdrew from the study after hearing this explanation.

A further complication arose from our assurances to parents and children that anything disclosed in interview would be kept confidential not only from outsiders (with the provisos noted earlier) but also from each other. This created some problems after the interviews. A few parents were clearly anxious to know what tales had been told or, more positively, to learn from what their child had said. For example, a drinking mother asked: 'Has he been telling you horrible stories about me?'. A partner in a different family asked more circuitously 'I know you can't really tell me, but is it possible to say if she's been badly damaged by it?' We explained that we could not say anything, since this would break the child's trust. In fact, only a few children were as hard on their parents as parents were themselves.

Parallel interviewing

The parallel interviewing system we adopted, with parents and child being seen simultaneously by two workers, had pros and cons, which may have implications for a potential counselling service with such families. Doing visits together was logistically convenient, saved on transport costs and, given the need to make evening visits in risky areas, provided an added element of safety. Families seemed comfortable with the arrangement; each party feeling they had someone to talk to, which may have reduced anxiety about what each was saying about the other.

On the other hand, it meant that both interviewers went into their interviews 'blind'. Fieldworkers were rightly anxious to preserve confidentiality and normally gave no information other than names, address and ages of children, and sometimes an indication of who the identified drinker was. The parent interviewer sometimes picked up crucial background information which, with hindsight, could have assisted the child interview (for example that a child had mild learning difficulties). Similarly, children sometimes raised issues which it might then have been possible to discuss with parents.

The value of understanding different perspectives

The rationale for holding separate interviews with parents and children was that this would give insights from different but complementary perspectives, a process known as triangulation in the research literature. Generally a more fruitful and comprehensive picture was obtained in this way than would have emerged from the interview of one party alone. For instance some children gave a fuller and more vivid description of parental drinking and its effects on themselves than their parents did. On the other hand, parents were often able to set these events in the context of the family history and the concerns of other family members. In a few cases the interviews yielded divergent or even conflicting interpretations of events, which led the interviewers into robust discussions, each identifying with their interviewee. These discussions were often valuable in helping to tease out the complexities of the situation. While, therefore, this report centres on children's experiences, we have sought to illuminate these by drawing equally on the accounts of both the children and their parents.

There were also gains from seeing siblings together. Each child could elaborate the descriptions provided by the other(s). When disagreements arose, these illuminated the divergent interpretations of family dynamics and the differential impact of drunkenness which can occur.

We would like to emphasise the value of the young adults' accounts. Time did not seem to have dimmed their vivid recollection. As with bereavement (Murray-Parkes, 1972), significant life events can be recalled with clarity many years later. At the same time, these respondents were in a position to evaluate and even reinterpret what had happened in the light of later experiences and adult understanding. This produced some interesting contrasts between children's and young adults' views on, for example, drink induced loving behaviour, which we refer to later (Chapter 4).

Special considerations in interviewing young children

Interviewing children calls for many of the skills used in talking with adults, but there are also some special emphases. The children's interviews demonstrated the increased significance of non-verbal communication for understanding children's perceptions and views. For instance, children regularly performed imitations of drunken behaviour and at times their facial expressions indicated sadness or disgust at parental drinking. Commonly a child used body language to accompany their verbal account of the physiological impact of alcohol consumption:

> *Interviewer* - What happens to people when they drink six glasses of that? (Pointing to picture of wine)
> *First child* - They get drunk
> *Interviewer* - Have you seen anybody who's drunk?
> *Second child* - Aye
> *First child* - A person in the shopping centre
> *Interviewer* - How did you know they were drunk? How can you tell when somebody is drunk?
> *First child* - 'Cause they were going from side to side (Child sways from side to side with arms outstretched)

The topics emphasised in interviews had to be adapted to their apparent relevance for the children concerned. For instance, children in one family maintained that their parents' drinking did not bother them, so that it was inappropriate to talk about needs for a service. In another interview with teenage siblings, they were more concerned about their father's depression than his drinking, so this was given particular attention.

With younger children especially, it was necessary to be very flexible in the order and nature of questioning. Some children were unable to remain stationary for long and provided their own agendas for the interview. This could be explained in a number of ways - in terms of the child's concentration, excitement at having undivided adult attention, reluctance to open up a sensitive subject or the artificial expectations of the research interview (Garbarino et al., 1992). To minimise the effects of this last factor, the purpose of the interviews was carefully explained and took place on the child's own territory. However, children at home then have the scope and confidence for diverting attention to their own possessions and interests. Respect for the child's wishes meant that it was occasionally important to spend time looking at a favourite book or toy, after which they could be coaxed back to the interview proper. At times, bargaining assisted this process, e.g. 'Come and sit down just now and we'll play the game when we have finished'.

Occasionally, children showed that they were tiring of the interview. When a young child was asked to talk further about his mother's drunkenness, he responded: 'Oh no! Not that again. I'm gonnae have a heart attack!'. Another child effectively ended the interview by announcing directly to the tape recorder:

> And now this special report is nearly finished. And now this is the TV News - and I'm a maniac!

Summary

The shame, secrecy and denial aroused by drinking problems meant that recruitment of families was the primary difficulty in this study. We have described in some detail the processes by which we gained access and the compromises made to the sampling and interviews, since similar considerations may be relevant to people establishing or running a service.

Intensive and proactive networking with a large number of agencies was needed in order to achieve the target sample of 20 cases of problem drinking families. The 27 children of these families ranged in age from 5 to 28, with two thirds being of school age. The families themselves represented a fair social mix. With the exception of the young adults, the respondent families were likely to have be more open in their communication and more positive in their relationships than is the case in many families with heavy drinking parents. Children and their parents were normally interviewed on one occasion only using a semi-structured outline. The fieldwork raised interesting issues relating to confidentiality, parallel interviewing, triangulation of different perspectives and communication with young children.

In the rest of the book, the children's experiences will be presented, drawing extensively on their own words and those of their parents. These portraits will then be supplemented by the views of professionals, after which we shall conclude by considering the implications for the development of services in this comparatively neglected area.

3 Problem drinking patterns

Introduction

Our aim had been to recruit families with problem drinking which showed a spread of types and severity. This was reasonably successful, though the procedures for identifying our sample resulted in the absence of very mild or unobtrusive problem drinking and that which is well concealed. Nevertheless the small sample exhibited a diverse range in the duration, timing and intensity of heavy drinking. This chapter outlines the main variations found in parental drinking patterns to lay the groundwork for subsequent chapters which consider their impact on children.

Location of drinking

In eight cases, the parent(s) drank outside the home, mainly in pubs, though mention was also made of 'garden parties' where drinkers congregate on street corners to share bottles of wine. In seven families, parent(s) drank mainly or exclusively at home, though some of them had started off as pub drinkers. In the remaining cases there was a mixed pattern.

Not surprisingly, men tended to drink outside the house whilst women, with greater child care responsibilities, usually drank at home, as Velleman and Orford (1990) also discovered. However, there seemed to be have been a common shift among men towards drinking more in the home once they married and had families. A typical progression followed by several was from furtive sharing of bottles of wine in the park as teenagers, to heavy drinking in pubs as young men, and then as fathers to bringing cans or bottles home to drink after the children were in bed. In one case, a father had stopped going to the pub at his wife's request, but continued to drink heavily at home.

Patterns of drinking

The timing and frequency of drinking is likely to have important consequences. Seilhamer et al. (1993) indicated that children are more adversely affected by their father's drinking when this occurs in the early evening - the usual 'prime time' for father-child interaction.

By examining the reported frequency, and timing of drinking, four main patterns were identified:

1. *Constant opportunistic drinking* (seven cases). These parents appeared to drink at any time of day, sometimes every day depending on finances, physical tolerance and particular stresses.

2. *Nightly drinking* (six cases) Consumption again occurred every day but only in the evenings, sometimes purposely so the children would be in bed and not witness it.

3. *Weekly heavy drinking* (two cases) Parents drank in a settled routine, either as a weekend 'treat' on Friday/Saturday evenings with Wednesdays as a mid-week boost or only on weekdays with the weekend as a sobering-up period. Some of the 'nightly' drinkers had also gone through a stage of doing this.

4. *Binge drinking* (three cases). Here bouts of drinking lasting days or weeks, during which parents drank most of the time, were followed by periods of complete sobriety. As the drinking problem worsened, the gaps between binges shortened. Although this was not a common pattern in the sample, many other drinkers occasionally went through a stage of it when they were repeatedly attempting and then failing to give up drinking altogether.

Constant and binge drinking took least account of children's routines, whereas some weekly and nightly drinkers did try to prevent their drinking interfering with their availability to their children.

There were also three modes of drinking - alone, with the partner or in the company of 'drinking pals'. This last mode of drinking was more likely to be regular and outside the home.

When both parents drank heavily there were two different patterns - joint drinking and separate drinking. In the latter type of family, it was more easy for one parent to remain available and supportive to the children, than when the two parents were drunk at the same time. In some ways, households with joint drinking couples resembled those with a lone parent drinker. During periods of heavy drinking, there was not another parent in a position to compensate and give support. On the other hand, there was also less adult conflict compared with two-parent households where one parent berated the other's drinking.

Behaviour when drunk

The children were given a prompt list of words to describe their parents' behaviour when drunk, and asked to choose ones they thought appropriate or suggest their own. A few selected positive or neutral words, like 'loving' and 'sleepy', but most chose negative terms. These included mad, smelly, cruel, angry, shouting, stupid, violent, bad-tempered and moody.

A more elaborate picture was built up by using a composite of information from parents, children and young adults. As would be expected, there was usually a marked and sometimes dramatic contrast between parents' behaviour when drunk and when sober. The phrase 'Jekyll and Hyde' occurred a number of times in interviews with parents and professionals to depict the sudden transformation from normal or positive behaviour to more negative manifestations, as if from a different person.

In four cases, the drinker's behaviour was seen as fairly neutral, though sometimes irritating. The parent became quiet and withdrawn when drunk. Slurred speech might occur. They were sometimes demanding but not particularly assertive and usually ended up just falling asleep.

In three families, drink seemed to have had overall positive effects. A depressed father visibly cheered up, for example. One mother became the life and soul of the party, another was genial and generous.

More often, however, the change was strongly negative. One mother was very ill, with DTs and shakes. Seven fathers became physically violent. In only three of these cases was violence to the children revealed and these were all young adults. It would obviously be difficult to obtain research interviews with children currently subject to violence. Hence in this sample it was mainly the other parent who was the recipient of the violence. In one instance the police were called out and in another family the mother and children had to escape from the house. A few violent drinkers, however, were said never to have assaulted their families, but instead turned their aggression onto non-human targets - smashing up the house or kicking the dog. In addition, five drinking parents (both mothers and fathers) though never physically violent, were verbally abusive to their children, sometimes to an extreme degree. Arguments between parents were common and sometimes had resulted in separations.

These crude categories, however, showed some overlap, particularly between the 'neutral' and 'positive'. Parents were often described as more loving when drunk, more generous with money, less 'narky', though other aspects of their behaviour were not regarded as positive. We return to this point later. Some parents' drinking started as neutral/positive and became negative later, either because the drinking worsened or the partner became more confrontational.

An important observation made by several families was that 'sobering up' after a drunken episode did not necessarily improve matters. Indeed a parent might be even worse than when drunk. For example, withdrawal symptoms or hangovers often made the parent irritable or intolerant of noise.

Norms about drinking

Rightly or wrongly, alcohol is part of our culture and problem drinking has to be seen in the context of what is considered 'normal' and socially acceptable. Therefore we asked about drinking expectations and patterns in the neighbourhood and family of origin, partly to see whether the identified drinker's imbibing appeared to be typical, exceptional or a more extreme version of local practice. This also provided glimpses of the variations in norms which exist according to family, neighbourhood and social class.

In certain areas of poor housing and high unemployment, some parents clearly regarded regular heavy drinking as a way of life, rather than a shameful secret. Three parents from these areas were drunk when seen and two continued to drink quite openly during their interviews. The other parent arrived late for interview fresh from the pub, drunk to the point of incoherence; none of the children in the family appeared embarrassed or attempted to cover up.

It appears that in certain areas a degree of heavy drinking is considered acceptable for men, particularly if it takes place in the evenings. Consequently it seems to create little embarrassment or need for secrecy. Several young adults described how most men in the streets where they lived regularly went to the pub at night, especially after getting their wages or benefit. On the other hand, it is considered less acceptable for women to drink heavily, especially during the day, and this can still be a taboo subject. One woman said her teenage son had been teased at school for having a mother who drinks.

There was an example of a different kind of heavy drinking norm in a middle class family. One of the young adults described her professional parents as having a lifestyle in which fairly heavy drinking was associated with party-going and entertaining among friends who all drank in similar fashion, though 'not horrendous quantities'. Apparently, in this context drinking was seen as equally acceptable for women as for men. Her mother was a great cook and regularly retired to the kitchen to concoct a meal accompanied by a bottle of wine.

One father living in a rural area said that the pub was the focus of community life there, an essential venue for social and practical networking:

> Even if you were totally teetotal, if you're dealing with anyone at all, you've got to go to the pub - as simple as that... You couldn't live in this village unless you all interacted in there - it's where everything gets done. If you want a chimney repaired and pick up the Yellow Pages, you might get a guy to do the job in a fortnight's time. If you want it done now, you go to the pub.

The image conveyed of this community was that very heavy drinking was common, leading to serious problems for some children, such as lacking money for food, being left alone in the house and exposed at parties to adult sex, drug-taking and fights. Compared to this, the father interviewed felt his five or six pints a night followed by a good sleep did not constitute a problem. This highlights the fact that definitions of drinking as problematic depend as much on expectations and the comparative context as on amount and effects.

A further 'normalising' factor for this man was the fact that all his family of origin also drank heavily. The transmission of problem drinking from one generation to another is well documented (Shucksmith 1994) not only in relation to drinkers but to their partners. It therefore came as no surprise that many of the identified drinkers in the sample and a high proportion of their non-drinking partners, came from such families. In the case of partners, it has been surmised that pathological patterns of response have been established in childhood, so that they seek out drinking partners to fulfil their own needs. However, a more straightforward explanation might be that partners who have grown up used to heavy drinking in the family have become desensitised to it and are therefore prepared to tolerate it in a partner, at least initially.

By contrast, someone brought up in a moderate or non-drinking household may draw the line at lower levels of heavy drinking, as the following couple illustrate:

> *Father* (identified drinker) - I think it's been agreed (by the clinic) that my wife's tolerance level is very low. So her levels and mine don't quite match. Whereas, if I was in someone else's house...
> *Mother* (from a teetotal family of origin) - See, this is the thing, he says: 'There's a lot of people worse than me' which I keep saying: 'Yes I know, but for this particular family, your behaviour's not acceptable.' Maybe somebody would be able to accept his behaviour, but personally, I can't and the children can't and they won't.

In order that problem drinking be perceived as abnormal, there may need to be a contrasting model available - within the family or in the neighbourhood. One young Primary child, with an extended family who drank only moderately, asked his mother critically why she drank beer, when his Dad drank coffee, tea and 'ginger'. Two young adults commented that in the quiet areas where they grew up there were few drinkers around, so their parents' drinking seemed particularly striking.

Recovery

Whereas 'sobering up' refers to emergence from a state of drunkenness, we use the term recovery to refer to the process of giving up alcohol misuse. Recovery may lead on to abstinence or controlled drinking. It may include periods of relapse and not uncommonly attempted recovery is unsuccessful.

We did not usually have access to any external evidence about current drinking in the sample. Based on the combined information of children and parents (including non-drinking partners) it seemed that half of the identified drinkers were either completely recovered or well on the way towards it. The periods of recovery ranged from 17 years to four weeks, but most were within the range of six months to one year. Some of these 'recovered' drinkers might well lapse later on. One of these parents was on a 'controlled drinking' regime - the others were all attempting to be completely abstinent.

The other drinking parents had made no recovery. In two cases (both parents of young adults) they seem to have received no help and died from drink-related illnesses. The remainder had been involved in recovery programmes, sometimes repeatedly over a period of years, but were still drinking heavily.

Summary

The drinking patterns revealed by the sample families were diverse and dynamic. Patterns could change in response to circumstances, including the onset of parenthood, or to attempts at recovery. Women tended to drink inside the home and men outside, though some men's drinking had become more home-centred once they married or had children. Certain parents drank whenever they could, day and night. A few drank heavily in bouts, with varying periods of sobriety between. More commonly there was some kind of routine with boundaries around the time of drinking - whether nightly or on one or more regular nights each week. When children were young, such drinking usually took place after they were in bed so was potentially or partially concealable from them.

Heavy drinking always resulted in altered parental behaviour. In a few cases, the change was portrayed as being mainly positive or neutral, but most parents became more aggressive or even violent when drunk. The unpleasantness could continue or even get worse during the sobering up phase.

The way in which the drinking was viewed by the drinker and other family members was much affected by the extent to which it could be seen as an extension of local norms or an individual aberration. Heavy drinking was sometimes rooted in and 'normalised' by similar patterns in the extended family or neighbourhood. In such circumstances, even a large alcohol intake could seem unproblematic. By contrast, the salience and disapproval of drinking were greater when it stood out from community or family traditions.

4 The direct impact on the child

Introduction: the dynamics of impact

The way that parental drinking affects children is highly complex. Various aspects of the child's situation interact with each other to produce different levels and time-scales of impact (Appendix 4). Parental drinking affects not only the child directly, but also other family members individually as well as the overall family dynamics which in turn influence the child. Parental drinking and its side-effects have an impact on children at two levels:

- the immediate emotional impact - how the situation makes them feel, which is in turn affected by their understanding of the alcohol consumption and its effects

- the long-term impact on personality, emotional well-being and social functioning

These are both mediated by the child's coping mechanisms and by the actions of significant others which may offset or exacerbate the effects of drinking.

Therefore in the ensuing four chapters we examine firstly the immediate direct impact of parental drinking on the child, then its consequences for the family as a whole. This is followed by consideration of coping and support, after which we review the long-term effects on the child of all these contributory factors. The present chapter deals with the direct impact of problem drinking behaviour and the repercussions of 'side-effects' of the drinking.

Immediate impact on the child of problem drinking behaviour

Children's understanding of alcoholic drinks and their consumption

Drinking parents sometimes claim their children know nothing about their drinking or are too young to understand it. This is part of the common tendency to underestimate children's capacities noted in Chapter 1. Previous research has shown that from an early age, children in general normally have an awareness of the distinction between alcoholic and non-alcoholic drinks, can identify drunken behaviour and usually disapprove of it (Fossey, 1994). Our study confirmed that children who live with problem drinking are indeed well aware of alcohol and its effects.

Even very young children in the sample recognised common alcoholic drinks, such as vodka, beer, wine and whisky and could distinguish them from non-alcoholic drinks:

> *Child 1* (looking at a prompt card) - Whisky. My mammy's got that, but it's a funny bottle.
> *Interviewer* (turns over next prompt card) - Do you know what that is?
> *Child 1* - Vodka.
> *Interviewer* (revealing further cards) - Do you know what that is?
> *Child 2* - Sherry (wine picture), Gin.
> Interviewer turns Coke card
> *Child 2* (shouting) - Cola!
> Interviewer - Is everybody allowed to drink these kinds of drinks?
> *Both children in unison* - No!
> *Child 2* - These the children should drink. (Coke and Tango)
> *Child 1* - And these, the adults (alcoholic beverages).

They all knew the effect of alcoholic drinks, too For example - 'They make you drunk'; 'They make you steamin'.

Many of the children, even the youngest, had already tried alcohol. Some were aware of differing views on this and the need for secrecy from those who disapprove. The mother of one young Primary boy came from a family who were members of Alcoholics Anonymous, whilst his paternal granny was said to encourage his father to drink:

> *Child* - Is that wine?
> *Interviewer* - Yes.
> *Child* - Yes, I like that.
> *Interviewer* - Do you like wine? Have you ever tasted wine?
> *Child* - Yes and I like the Tango.
> *Interviewer* - When did you taste this one? (pointing to the picture of wine).

Child - I tasted it from when I was three.
Interviewer - Where did you taste it?
Child - Just around here.
Interviewer - Did you? Did any grown up know you were tasting it?
Child - My Gran. But my Mum never. (whispers) My Gran never told my Mum.
Interviewer - Did she not? (also whispers) Was it just between you and your Gran?
Child - Aha.
Interviewer - Did you say you liked it?
Child - Aha.
Interviewer - Is everybody allowed to drink those kind of drinks?
Child (placing wine and Tango cards together) - That's the ones I like.

All the children in the sample including the youngest acknowledged in the interviews that their parent(s) drank alcohol and most alluded to situations of drunkenness. They were neither ignorant of the drinking, nor did they try to conceal it. For instance:

Interviewer - Have you ever seen anybody drunk in your family?
Child 1 - Aha. My Mum and Dad. My Dad last night. Was it Saturday night?
Child 2 - Aye.

They also realised clearly that the consumption of alcohol altered physical states and behaviour, both in their parents and outsiders. They could competently recognise direct and indirect effects, as the same two Primary children illustrate:

Child 1 - Saturday night - he went back - he was going like this (child sways) He stood on the dog's paw.
Child 2 - And he was going 'Ooooh! Oooh! (simulates a dog howling)
Interviewer - The dog was....
Child 1 - Yelping.
Interviewer - Any other things that told you your dad was drunk?
Child 1 - He had smelly breath.
Child 2 - And he was sick in bed.

When questioned, another young child was able to make the link between his mother's drinking and her hospitalisation:

Interviewer - Did you know what was wrong with your Mummy?
Child - Aha. She was sick.

> *Interviewer* - She was sick. Sometimes people have different sorts of sicknesses - do you know what kind of sickness it was?
> *Child* - Maybe she was.... Aye! (with emphasis) I know how it is noo. 'Cause she was drinking beer.

Children gave reasons why their parents drank which usually coincided well with parental accounts. They did not see it as an arbitrary phenomenon or a personality problem, but showed a good appreciation of the factors which can contribute to problem drinking. Their attributions were mainly couched in terms of parents responding to stress, though drinking was also sometimes referred to as a habit. The stresses mentioned were related to marital discord, depression, bereavement, financial worries and self-blame. In other words the children's explanations were largely social and environmental, rather than physiological or medical:

> He was only drinking because he was depressed all the time. It was the only way he could get away from everything.

> He deserved a drink (laughter) after working all week, cause you can see him getting worse and worse, just getting tired and all that and coming home on Friday night..

> My Ma and Da used to have a fight noo and again. He used to hit her bad and ma Ma used to hit him bad but ma Ma said it was because ma Da was hitting her. That's what's made her drink noo, but she's been drinking like that for 14 years

Unusually, one Primary child simply saw heavy drinking as a pleasurable pursuit which adults engage in for its own sake:

> To get drunk and plus they enjoy themselves - cause sometimes they need a break from different children. Sometimes they get bored like my Aunt Pat!

It has been comonly reported that young children tend to blame themselves for parental drinking, often explaining this in terms of Piaget's ideas that they are likely to think of themselves as causing events which in fact have other origins (Velleman, 1995). In our study, there was little evidence of children blaming themselves for the drinking as such, although a few of the young adults said this was a phase they had passed through before recognising the adults were responsible. However, a third of the children did express feelings that their behaviour was sometimes to blame for triggering drinking episodes. Two boys in different households articulated the view that they were 'bad' or engaged in stealing because their mother drank, yet they also recognised that she turned to drink when upset about their behaviour. Two sisters admitted that on occasion they blamed themselves for their father's drinking, because he stormed off to the garden shed for a drink when they had done something wrong. A Secondary girl said:

> She drinks when she's under pressure and we're really cheeky and we don't help a lot. I think I should help more in the house.

It is possible that some children may generalise such feelings of responsibility for particular incidents to the drinking as a whole.

Emotional impact - how the children felt about heavy drinking

Some children viewed their parents' heavy drinking with amusement or indifference, though negative responses were more commonly reported.

Positive impact

In our interviews, we sought to be open-minded about the possible consequences of heavy drinking and to avoid the common assumption that it is inevitably problematic for children. As it turned out, some children did speak about aspects they recalled as enjoyable. A few of the younger children clearly found drunken behaviour funny:

> *Child 1* - One day my Auntie Margaret came up to ma house a couple of days after New Year and they all got drunk.
> *Child 2* - And we stayed and ma Mum was trying to get me (and my cousins) in the same bed and she was telling us - she was like that 'Freddie's going to get you' (the character from 'Nightmare on Elm Street').
> *Child 1* - And ma Uncle Eddie fell.
> *Child 2* - And he was drunk and he got a carpet burn (both laugh).

Two Secondary girls described how their father, who drank to relieve his depression, became markedly happier when drunk.

Parents could become more generous with money:

> *Interviewer* - How can you tell your Mum's drunk?
> *Child* - Cause she keeps on getting us up and giving us money.
> *Interviewer* - Does she give you money?
> *Child* - Aye - pounds!

Children might enjoy the freedom from adult control:

> It's a bit hard to explain - I don't know. I don't get put to bed early (laughter) and they don't come in and check you. You can do anything in the room... and we just go in the room and they buy us and give us money and we go down to the van and get sweets and things and juice. That's us - we just keep ourselves happy (last sentence said in a jolly tone).

Whilst initially and at the time this can seem beneficial, a few of the young adults offered a different perspective. They pointed out how this could develop into lack of supervision or interest in school-work, which might contribute to poor performance at school, non-attendance or even more serious behaviour problems.

Three of the Primary children spoke approvingly of the fact that their parents became more loving when drunk:

> *Child* - Every time they're drunk they say 'Come here' and give me cuddles. And I sit on their knee and they hold me tight and don't let me go.
> *Interviewer* - Who are you talking about?
> *Child* - My Mum and my aunties - everybody in the house... My Dad sits in that chair (by the fire) and I sit on the floor between his legs and I sit like that.
> *Interviewer* - Is that when he's drunk and when he's not drinking as well?
> *Child* - When he's not drunk and when he's really drunk (emphasis) you canna get away from him (laughs). They cuddle you all the time - they keep hold of you (laughs).

However, loving behaviour of this kind may likewise undergo some reinterpretation as the child matures. Two of the young adults spoke critically of what they now regarded as false affection induced by the alcohol . Hence one young man said his mother would be 'overbearingly' loving in a drunken way which made him draw back. A young woman expressed ambivalence, too:

> I know for a fact that I was loved more than a lot of people I know, affection-wise. Flowed to us in unyielding levels and sometimes that was more confusing, because you would be fighting with somebody and your defences would be up and you'd say 'I hate you' you know, 'I don't want to be your friend anymore' sort of thing and then you would kiss them goodnight, right? I hear people say 'My Mum and Dad never cuddled me' and I've thought, God, they smothered me, they loved me so much!

The implication that the physical demonstrativeness may derive from the parent's need for closeness rather than a wish to nurture the child, was sharply pointed out by one Primary boy:

> *Interviewer* - Can you tell me about the loving?
> *Child* - They go like that (child hugs himself and adopts an intense and louder tone) and cuddle me and all that.
> *Interviewer* - And what do you think of that?
> *Child* - Horrible.
> *Interviewer* - Do you not like it? Does it embarrass you?
> *Child* - Aye. (short laugh)
> *Interviewer* - Don't you like getting cuddles?
> *Child* - (shakes head)
> *Interviewer* - Are you not a cuddly type of person?
> *Child* - I'm not a cuddly toy.

This quotation illustrates how children could resent being treated like an object, even if the parent was superficially being affectionate. Fahlberg (1994) has suggested that repeated behaviour on the part of a parent or carer which disregards the child's wishes and reactions is likely to generate anxiety or emotional distancing in the child.

Nevertheless a few children in the sample did seem to enjoy their parents' loving behaviour when drunk and value should be accorded to this expressed view in its own right. We cannot assume that the contrasting view of some young adults represents a natural progression, because it may be that their experiences were just different.

Indifference

A few of the children seemed to be little affected one way or another by their parents' heavy drinking. When parents did their drinking outside the home or returned after the children were in bed and then simply went to sleep, children seemed untroubled by it. One mother (who was the identified drinker) had a long history of binge drinking which involved her disappearing for days or weeks at a time. However, her Primary age children, while recognising that she drank alcohol, did not apparently see it as a problem. They focused instead on their father's occasional but more dramatic sprees. Significantly they viewed only their father's drinking as 'worrying'. This was confirmed and explained by their parents' accounts:

> *Mother* - I just have a fag and go to sleep... The weans don't normally see me, do they?
> *Father* - Na, I've always got them in their beds sleeping.
> *Interviewer* - Do you think it worries them at all?
> *Mother* - Don't think so - doesn't bother them, does it Alex?

> *Father* - Naw, they don't bother, long as their Pa's wi' them. (Both parents laugh)
> *Interviewer* - When you go away for a while, does that bother the girls?
> *Father* - That first time it did.
> *Mother* - Aye.
> *Father* - They don't bother now... They know everything they want, I'll give it them, so they're no caring!!

Here, the lack of impact was apparently due to the absence of any associated problematic behaviour combined with the availability of a second carer. However, more dramatic behaviour could also be taken in a child's stride, when it was regarded as normal. Two young adults whose father was regularly very drunk and occasionally violent illustrate this point:

> *Young Adult 1* - I mean I've seen him walking up the street and people are helping him up the stairs and bringing him to the door
> *Interviewer* - Why do some families keep it secret?
> *Young Adult 2* - Maybe they're ashamed.
> *Interviewer* - Are you ever?
> *Both* - No.
> *Young Adult 1* - I mean that's the way he wants to live, fair enough. As long as it doesnae interfere wi' our lives and as long as he doesnae start his crap again.

The drinking was certainly not seen as positive here, but neither was it markedly negative. It was more of an irritation which has to be lived with.

Negative impact

However, most children were in no doubt that heavy drinking is unpleasant. The children in the sample were asked to put into words how they felt when their parents were drinking. Younger children were assisted by written prompts. Nearly all chose negative expressions (they often selected two or three):

Table 4.1
Children's responses to drunken behaviour

Worried	6
Angry	5
Frightened	5
Upset	4

Sad, depressed	4
Puzzled	2
Excited	2
Neglected	1
Happy	1

These mostly show helplessness and unhappiness, although there were some who expressed active anger.

For many children, drinking had objectionable sensory associations, like smelly breath or the smell of alcohol itself, as this young Primary child describes:

> *Child* - On that *night* at Christmas go shut with ma eyes and the stink when everybody went away.
> *Interviewer* - The stink?
> *Child* - With all the beer and the whisky, everybody was drinking it. It was a *horrible* party. I wasnae in it. I was just sitting outside (in a fed up tone) The stupid people was doing it.
> *Interviewer* - And you didn't like the smell of the drinks?
> *Child* - I didnae like it.

This child's story also illustrates another negative aspect of parental drinking: his account shows that he felt excluded from this adult activity. Another drinking parent explains how this can arise when the adults are pre-occupied:

> I feel as if they think you're no' concentrating on them, you know? See if you're drinking, you get locked up in one another...

The child's perspective on this was vividly conveyed by a young adult:

> He treated us as if we were invisible. The focus of his attention was the drink and was to get drunk.

In these cases, the parent was emotionally absent, but drink can of course also result in physical separation. Two of the mothers in the sample were sometimes absent from home when drunk. In one case this appeared to cause little distress after the first occasion because the second parent was there to look after the children. However, in the other case, the mother was the sole carer and her absences often overnight, caused considerable upset to her oldest son.

This was the only child in the sample who spontaneously used the word 'neglect', by which he meant not having enough to eat. Many of the others stressed that despite other faults, their parents had always provided a basic level of care, with enough food, reasonable clothing and sometimes sacrifices made to ensure they could take part in activities such as school trips. A Secondary boy said his mother, who was the identified drinker, had always bought him clothes. A young man compared his childhood favourably in material terms with that of others living around him - 'there was always food on the table'. Sometimes the household was kept going largely because of efforts to compensate by a non-drinking parent, but it was also clear that a number of the identified drinkers were also able to sustain basic responsibilities. Indeed, providing an adequate level of physical care was a point of pride with many of the drinking parents and their children (a fact which may, incidentally, make it harder to identify the children as having problems). However, in concentrating on fulfilling this basic parental requirement, some parents did not realise that their children were missing out on attention, affection or emotional security. The following exchange with a very drunk father makes the point:

> *Interviewer* - So really, you think your kids haven't been affected by your drinking?
> *Father* - Do my kids look hungry?
> *Interviewer* - No they don't.
> *Father* - Do they look starved?
> *Interviewer* - They don't, no. Do you think they've been worried by it at all?
> *Father* - No.

So far, we have considered the negative impact caused by parent absence (physical, psychological, emotional). However, most commonly the perceived negative impact occurred when parents were present and resulted from the change in behaviour which alcohol brought about. Children spoke of silliness, carelessness, clumsiness and irritating behaviour. At the mildest end of the spectrum parents were described by their children as 'stupid'. One 'talks a load of rubbish'; another 'yabbers on and talks a load of junk.' One parent left lights on so the child couldn't get to sleep.

Parents might also become demanding, annoying or embarrassing, for example by 'asking for 20 cups of tea' or making a more public scene:

> When she's walking along the road and I'm wi' her and she hasn't got a fag and she asks somebody and they say 'No, I'm no' gi'ing you one' she'll start arguing and all that wi' em. It's mad.

Much of this behaviour contradicts expectations concerning adulthood, maturity and especially the parental role - a point we shall return to. Usually it did not appear to be deeply upsetting, but some young adults remarked on the cumulative effect of shame and resentment. However, the majority of children faced more serious problems.

Undoubtedly, the most common and most serious problem for children in our sample was drunken violence. The majority of parents became aggressive when drunk, which was very frightening for most children. The aggression took different forms. A few young adults had experienced physical violence against themselves. In one instance this was of a horrific nature, though drink seemed to be only one factor in the abuse:

> *Young adult* - When they had a drink they took it out on me.
> *Interviewer* - Was it just when they were drinking that you got battered?
> *Young adult* - No, sober as well. I was tied to a chair, tied up by the wrists - that's how bad it was. You know that sheep-dip stuff, you know, poisonous stuff, I had that poured down my throat as well. That was all through my step-mum. She egged my Dad on, you know what I mean. That still hurts me a lot. I've only told yourself and one other. Another time as well, I had my wrist broke. That was with a spanner, one of those heavy duty spanners. That was my Dad coming back.

The children interviewed did not mention incidents when they had been physically ill-treated. However, it should be borne in mind that if any child had been the victim of physical violence, they were unlikely to reveal this when other family members were in the next room.

Quite common, though, were reports that the children had witnessed violence against the other parent or the home. This represented a frightening threat to the person and place which normally provide a strong sense of security for children. A young man vividly remembered his experiences:

> It was horrible. He'd go aboot like a raging bull. He tried to stab ma Ma, they stabbed each other wi' knives and all that. It was mad.

The father of two Primary children was regularly violent to their mother and here they recount an incident which had clearly been distressing:

> *Child 1* - (points to the word 'violent' on behaviour prompt sheet)
> *Child 2* - He wasn't violent a lot. When we were in bed sometimes.
> *Interviewer* - How did you know?
> *Child 1* - Because we woke up.
> *Child 2* - And we were in bed and we heard ma Mum shouting 'his name.
> *Child 1* - And we thought it was me.
> *Child 2* - And Davie ran in and I just followed him.

Interviewer - Did you know what was going on when you were in your bedroom?
Child 1 - My Mum had a big bruise on her face and big bruise on her leg.
Interviewer - How did you used to feel?
Child 1 - (very quickly answers without visual probes) Horrible, angry and upset
Interviewer - (shows the children the 'feelings' prompts)
Child 1 - (immediately points to 'upset')
Interviewer - I can imagine that you would feel very upset
Child 2 - (points to 'frightened') The way he was punching and the shouting.
Child 1 -(points to 'worried') I didn't know what was going to happen to us but then we went to a refuge.
Child 2 - I was worried when we were in the refuge as well.

Their non-drinking mother describes the same incident from her viewpoint:

He punched me on the head while I was sleeping. I sat up 'What are you doing?' and he was shouting abuse at me. All I remember is Davie and Tracy pulling and screaming. He came for me at that point and I don't remember anything except for they two screaming and shouting and pulling him off me. And I got up and said 'Come on, it's all OK' and went into the room and shut the door. He was shouting his head off and calling me names and everything. Davie and Tracy were terrified that night and we were in bed and Tracy was absolutely shaking with fright. I was thingmy myself, right enough and he kept shouting he was going to kill me and put me in a box, a blood bath and all this. We were terrified. I just sat holding them on Tracy's bed, trying to calm them down and he came back, slamming the door wide open and shouting and then slamming it shut. This went on for about an hour, then he went to his bed.

However, despite the trauma experienced in relation to the violence, the children were also able to recognise another aspect of their father's drinking:

Child 1 - But he still loved us when he was drunk, but....
Child 2 - He wasn't' always like that. Sometimes he could be silly and all that.

It seems that circumstances can influence the manifestation of drunken behaviour, a point made by the children's mother. She described how he used to come in drunk and:

They saw it as funny. He gave them a cuddle - they saw it as just the normal thing. It was only when they started to see him violent (that they were scared) and that was because I was starting to stand up to him.

This illustrates how, when a woman justifiably asserts her own rights, the drinker can respond in manner which makes things worse for the children.

Clearly, incidents like this are not only very frightening at the time, but deeply trouble children. When explaining how parents and children are affected differently by drinking, a Primary boy said:

Child - My Mum was affected by getting hit and all that and we were affected inside.
Interviewer - Are you saying your Mum got hit and it hurt?
Child - Ma Mum got hurt on the outside and we got hurt in the inside.

Violence was not always directed at people. Several drinkers displaced their aggression and frustration onto objects in the house, sometimes deliberately. The father of one Primary boy explains how this occurred and empathised with his son's distress:

I smashed that wall, I smashed the window... I was losing ma temper but I didna want to hit (my wife), so I took it oot on the wall and the window. He seen that happening and he was screaming. It's a nightmare every time I think of it. It hurts me inside because I know how much it must have hurt him.

His son gave his own account to the interviewer one year on, this time recollected in comparative tranquillity:

Child - I'll tell you a good story. The police was in the house.
Interviewer - The police were in the house - were they?
Child - In ma house.
Interviewer - Were they?
Child - Aha.
Interviewer - Why was that?
Child - Because ma Dad smashed the window because he was drunk.
Interviewer - So when he was drunk he smashed a window?
Child - Aha.
Interviewer - So what did you think about that?
Child - I was crying. I had to go and stay wi' ma Gran that night.
Interviewer - Did you?
Child - The room was freezing.
Interviewer - Because all the air was getting in the window?

> *Child* - Aha, ma Mum was (makes sound of short frightened breath) panicking in case the door was gonna fall over her head.

Although physical violence against children was rarely reported by children in our sample, they frequently spoke of verbal abuse. This consisted of denigration, name-calling and threats, which they found very distressing. One Secondary girl said her mother shouted and threatened when drunk, making her feel unwanted, sad and cross:

> When she says 'You're going into a home' I know she'll never do it. She says things to me ... It's terrible, I don't feel like staying here. I feel like going to stay with my Gran or my friend.

A Secondary boy reported intense humiliation by his mother, when she was drunk. This was made worse by what he saw as the absence of any provocation whatsoever on his part:

> She can bring me doon to all sorts of sizes. She just done it a couple of nights ago. Ma pals were sitting in the bedroom and ... she comes in (and shouts) 'Everyone of yous - oot!'. Nobody's done nothing to her, you know what I mean?

Similarly in another family a father tormented his older daughter (of Secondary age) when drunk, using unpleasant names like 'Ignorant bastard'; 'Fat lazy slob' and other worse names she did not want to reveal. This often reduced her to tears and occasionally to a state of panic.

> Like, one night I got really bad and I couldn't breathe properly. I was like - Aah, Aah, Aah (simulates gasping for breath). I was really, really bad and Mum was going to phone the doctor, but I was calmed down. But anytime I sorta calmed down a wee bit better, then he'd call me a name again and then I went to ma bed. It does, it gets you upset, the things that he does and says about you.

When asked to sum up the impact of their father's drinking, this girl said: 'Ever since I can remember I've been scared. It's affected us all our lives.'

So far we have considered the impact on children of the drunken behaviour. For the most part this was experienced as unpleasant and distressing in itself, but when heavy drinking is persistent other problems arise which also affect children's lives in major ways. The rest of the chapter is concerned with how children felt about such knock on effects of the drinking.

Family dislocation

Marital conflict is a common by product of problem drinking (See also chapter 5). Many of the children referred with feeling to arguments, even where they had not involved violence. When disputes led to separations, the impact could be as distressing to children as the actual behaviour which provoked them, if not more so. After a violent incident when their father was drunk, two children went to a Women's Refuge with their mother. According to her, they hated losing their home and were very unhappy in the Refuge. Moving schools was a further disruption for them. The children felt they were no longer a family - other children talked about their Dads and they couldn't. With hindsight, the mother concluded that the separation had affected them far more than the original drinking.

As in this case, several families had experienced several moves of home and school following family division. This interrupted learning and disrupted friendships, as this young woman explained:

> Cause we used to live in all different places and all different houses and all that. And they started and all that the same kind of ways and all that. Different places and different houses and all that as well.

Financial problems

Interestingly, severe money problems did not figure as prominently as might have been expected in parental descriptions of the difficulties that drinking can cause, including the accounts by partners of identified drinkers. While it is possible this was affected by taboos about discussing money matters with outsiders, most parents did show a readiness to talk about other sensitive matters. More probably then, for most of this particular group of families the financial consequences of heavy drinking appeared less salient than the other more traumatic effects.

Nevertheless significant money issues were mentioned spontaneously by several parents, for whom it was a major concern. The financial difficulties took different forms, depending on income level and life-style. In one family there were arguments about use of a visa card and a bank overdraft, whilst in others money spent on drink from the Income Support book left the family desperately short of cash. One family had lost their house because of the drinking father's failure to pay the mortgage and two had taken out unmanageable loans because of debts to which the drinking contributed.

Four children and three young adults referred directly to shortage of cash as a problem. One said: 'My Mum's always skint - she borrows money off of us'. Some of their drawings and their wishes for the future referred to money, although they may be no different from other children of non-drinking parents in that respect. Examples of the problems mentioned by children included a father spending on drink money which had been set aside to pay for household bills and a Secondary boy saying he could not trust his mother with money for fear she would use it for drink. Another Secondary boy recounted how his mother exchanged benefit books with his father to finance her drinking:

> Ma Da used to get his Monday money, lend it ma Ma till Tuesday, then ma Ma gave ma Da the book on Tuesday. Ma Da used to give her the full money on the Monday and she used to have it done by the Monday night.

A young man recollected:

> I used to wait until he fell asleep when he was drunk and gae in and steal money out of his pockets and gi' it to ma Ma, because he was always drinking it. He was getting all his wages and blowing it all on drink.

All four children in the group discussion agreed that shortage of money was a problem. They also complained about broken promises to get new trainers or go out for a meal, because parents had drunk the money intended for that.

Thus, overall, shortage of money was a significant worry for some children in the sample, but in most instances it did not seem to cause the same degree of anxiety and trauma as other aspects of drinking.

Sobering up and recovery

One side-effect of heavy drinking which had an unexpected impact on children was cessation of the drinking. For some children, non-drinking periods could be just as traumatic as drunken episodes. The withdrawal symptoms which drinkers experienced made them morose, bad-tempered or sensitive to disturbance. One mother who was an exceptionally heavy drinker experienced serious symptoms which troubled her Secondary age son greatly until he became familiar with the process:

> *Boy* - She wakes up in the morning with shakes and all that.
> *Interviewer* - How do you feel when you've seen your Mum like that?

Boy - Terrified. I was at first but I'm used to it now. She gets all twitchy and all that. She's had DT's and all that - you hallucinate - she's had all that...

These extreme physical effects were uncommon in our sample, but other children did describe hangovers and withdrawal in negative terms. A young woman whose father drank only during the week much preferred him drunk to sober:

See at the weekends when he's no drinkin', he's dead narky, he's pure murder to live wi' - he's dead quick tempered. Just the slightest wee thing, he goes pure mad - his eyeballs jump oot his heid an that! It's worse when he's no' drinking.

Where a parent had a regular drink pattern like this, the children in effect never saw them other than drunk or hungover. On the other hand, when a parent drank only in bouts with long gaps in between, there was time for the other more positive dimensions of the parent to emerge. One Secondary girl had a warm, involved relationship with her father during his sober periods, when 'he's the best Dad anyone could have and I can talk to him if I've got a problem'. Even so, with bout drinkers uncertainty was a problem for the children. Since parents had stopped before only to start again after a while, there was a constant anxiety even in the sober periods that the drink problems would return, as another Secondary girl pointed out:

Girl - Like I used to worry even when he wasn't drinking - like he would stop for a few months. I would still worry even then.
Interviewer - Was that to do with him starting again?
Girl - Aha.

Recovery from alcohol misuse was longed for by most children in the sample, all but a few of whom expressed a wish for this without prompting. Children who had experienced it were warm in their praises of the abstinent parent. One Secondary boy distinguished between his mother temporarily not drinking and completely abstinent for a period: '(When she's) aff it for a good while you can get into a routine of talking to her more than when she's drunk'. Another portrayed his mother as 'a totally different person' when in a detox unit. A third vividly described his recently abstinent mother: 'She's brand spanking new'.

However, recovery can itself pose new problems for the child. For instance:

- lax parents tightened up discipline and demands

- drinkers had to expend a lot of emotional energy on their efforts to stay off alcohol permanently, which reduced what they could give to their children

- individual counselling sessions and attendance at therapeutic groups took up time, so children received less attention

- other psychological and emotional problems previously masked by alcohol emerged and had to be coped with

- reconciliation between previously warring partners could mean the child felt excluded

One father was acutely aware of these problems for his young son:

> I just find that the last year I've been so much self-centred ... but noo I'm trying to think of everybody else as well... And another thing I find is, because of the amount of attention I paid to him all the time, me and his mother are getting on better, so I think he's jealous. Because he sees me and his mother getting on. He doesnae like us sitting beside each other. Because before, we weren't getting on, we were arguing every night.

Another couple pursued the same theme:

> *Father* - I would say that (my wife) and I started to get closer and (my wife) would maybe be paying me mair attention than she had in the past as well and the children would resent that.
> *Mother* - Especially Joanne. She would always say 'What're you sookin' up to him for?' and you had to stand and say 'Well, look, I love you but I also love him' you know?

Emotional distress in context

The evidence is clear from this study that although heavy drinking can sometimes be regarded by children as harmless and even fun, more commonly its impact is seen as negative, often acutely so. What we cannot provide is any sense of how this compares with the emotional effects on children of other significant life events. Nearly all children will experience trauma to varying degrees at some point in their lives. These include parental arguments, separations, loss of close friendships because of moving home or 'falling out', peer group teasing, bullying, parental anger or punishment, serious illness or death of a close relative (Hill et al., 1995). For at least some of the children in our sample, drinking seemed to be less emotionally salient than other significant events. When children were asked what was the worst thing that had happened to them, some mentioned parental drinking but others cited the death of a grandparent, or a close cousin; their father's depression; a spell in foster care; parental separation. Each of these can happen to children without drinking problems.

In emphasising the distress that is caused to children by parental drinking and in searching for ways to alleviate it, we should not lose sight of the fact that other aspects of their lives also cause distress and may also need attention.

Summary

Contrary to the expectations of some of the parents, the children were knowledgeable about alcohol and its effects from an early age. Even quite young children in the sample were familiar with alcoholic drinks and most of the sample had tried them. All were well aware that their parents drank heavily. Moreover, the children were able to offer explanations for the drinking which took account of situational and chronic stresses in their parents' lives. They recognised that social as well as personal factors contributed to the drinking patterns.

The emotional impact of parental drinking included positive aspects such as fun, good humour and loving behaviour. However, for the majority of children the main impact was negative, although a number had experienced other events which they viewed as equally or more distressing. The direct effects of drunken behaviour included physical, emotional or psychological withdrawal, unpredictability, and witnessing or experiencing physical or verbal violence. Indirect consequences included separations, multiple changes of address and financial problems. Some changes associated with periods of abstaining also created difficulties.

As we have begun to see, the effects of drinking were usually intermingled with other aspects of the family situation. These are explored more fully in the next chapter.

5 Impact of the drinking on family dynamics with indirect consequences for the child

Introduction

Children do not just respond to parental drinking in isolation. Both the drinking and children's reactions are part of a complex set of interrelationships and activities within the household.

The impact of problem drinking on the operation of family relationships is widely recognised in the literature. There are references to children taking physical and psychological responsibility for parents, alliances forming against the identified drinker and the family closing itself off from outsiders to preserve the drinking as a secret (Fanti, 1990). Sometimes the family is portrayed as a 'system' in which actions by any one part of the system (family member) is affected by and in turn affects not only other individual parts of the system, but also the operation of the family 'system' as a whole (Orford, 1985; Dallos, 1995). Whilst this analogy can become too mechanistic, the core idea is helpful one, namely that there is a constant interplay within a family between particular actions or events and the wider set of relationships. Any action or change by one person in the family has repercussions for everyone else. This approach to understanding families emphasises the importance of the ways in which boundaries affecting communication and interaction are maintained within the family, as well as between the family and the outside world. A further key concept is that of circular causality, where one person's behaviour can both 'cause' and be 'caused by' the behaviour of others in a cyclical process. We were to find this has relevance to the interplay between parental drinking and children's behaviour.

In this chapter, we look at these effects and others in the families in our sample. Family dynamics interact with children's coping, which is dealt with in the next chapter, so the two should be viewed together. This chapter concentrates on parent-child relationships, whilst sibling interaction is described in chapter 6, but it must be remembered that these two aspects of family dynamics also affect each other.

We begin with one of the central features of families where a parent drinks heavily. The parent's ability to fulfil general expectations of adult caring roles within the family is reduced or altered. As a result, the children may not only miss out on some of the care, attention and responsiveness normally given by parents, but may themselves have to take on certain of the practical or emotional responsibilities typically regarded as more appropriate for parents in our society.

Children looking after parents, siblings or the home

The most obvious examples occur when a child regularly takes on major domestic responsibilities like taking sole charge of cooking, cleaning, doing the laundry, getting younger children off to school. This issue has been highlighted recently in relation to 'young carers', children with parents who are physically disabled (Aldridge and Becker, 1995). Their circumstances are often depicted and sometimes experienced as exploitative, but we need to recognise that in other societies many or all children are expected to carry out such tasks from a much earlier age than in Britain (Weisner and Gallimore, 1977; Ross and Bergum, 1990). This is sometimes seen as offering children opportunities to develop competence and take part in the adult world, not as an undue imposition. It is important to remember, too, that when children do take on major caring tasks, they usually continue to receive other forms of support and guidance from parents (Reed, 1995). There are dangers of generalising from a situations where children take on some practical tasks normally carried out by parents to talk of role reversal which seems to imply that all aspects of parenting have been transferred to the child. Keith and Morris (1995) have been critical of the trend to portraying children of disabled parents as 'young carers', heroic and overburdened, which ignores all the positive contributions of the parents to their children.

In relation to parents with drink problems, it is quite possible for children to assume some practical or emotional responsibilities for a drunken parent or to undertake tasks the parent is incapable of. However, in many instances the other parent is quite willing and able to look after children and the home, whilst heavy drinkers may still be able to perform parental functions, especially when sober. As a result, constant practical 'role reversal' did not seem to be common in our sample. We heard of instances of this from professionals and one Secondary girl in the group discussion had sometimes assumed these responsibilities. She said she felt like a mother to her siblings. One of our young adults spoke of his older sister doing the cooking as a child when his mother was drunk. However there were no other examples of this in our sample, and nearly all the parents appeared to have been able to maintain a basic level of care with support from partners or extended family. Where children did mention household responsibilities of any kind, it was in terms of helping the parent in a way that would be considered routine in most families: minding a younger child for a few hours or helping with the housework. In effect, it seemed that when the drinking parent was out of action, there was either a sober partner to cope or else the household duties were simply abandoned for the time being.

However, the children as well as the young adults in our sample were involved in occasional caring for their parents in other ways. For example one Primary girl said she physically supported her parents when they were staggering: 'When my Mum's drunk, I always walk her - I always walk her and help her. And sometimes my Dad as well'. Her older sister reported accompanying her father when he was really drunk in case he was mugged. She also helped him with his debts. Another young adult recalled trying to take on the family's financial problems to help her mother, with little success:

> She used to tell me all her problems - how they had money difficulties. I used to sit and say 'Right, I'll work it oot. I know how much we get a week, we'll pay this and we'll pay that and that'll be fine.' But it never worked out like that, I could never tell her - I was only a wean.

Night-time seemed to be a peak period for children's caring role. One young Primary boy described trying to help his mother to bed:

> *Child* - I was carrying her and then I fell.
> *Interviewer* - You were carrying your Mummy?
> *Child* - Aye. When she's trying to go to bed, she walks like this (He stands up and simulates swaying from side to side). Then I held her and then I fell and then I'm greetin'.

A young adult also recalled putting her father to bed:

> I can remember maybe about three years ago, it was really bad, the violence. I was arguing with him and I went to put him to his bed. It was Christmas time and we had a lot of friends and that in and neighbours and when they've got a drink in them their minds just goes and they say what they want to say. He started wi' all this abuse. I just said, 'Right, time for bed' and put him to his bed.

A Secondary boy had occasionally slept at his mother's side when she had D.T.s to stop her wandering at night:

> *Boy* - When she had the DT's I used to go into bed with her and all that so she could get a sleep instead of getting up and walking about and seeing things and all that.
> *Interviewer* - Did you have to hold her to keep her in the bed?
> *Boy* - My bed's like this one at the wall (referring to bed he is sitting on which is against the wall) and I used to lie at the front so she couldnae get out. When she got up in the morning she still had the DTs.

In the main then, children in these families mainly took over the temporary care of and assistance to their parents, rather than full household responsibilities. They acted much as a parent might to a sick child.

Children as protectors

Children in our sample were also involved in protecting one parent from the other, usually the mother from the father. One young woman when younger had physically intervened to prevent her violent father from attacking her mother, occasionally getting hurt in the process. A mother of Primary children indicated that they had protected her on occasion from her husband's violence. They tried to pull him off her and he was so disturbed by their hysterical screaming, that 'they made him back off'. At least once when she was badly frightened she asked them to stay with her for protection.

One of the drinking mothers in the study had been used as a psychological shield herself when a child:

> I was always put between my Mum and Dad. My Dad, if he took a drink ... she put me there so my Dad wouldn't do anything. ... I've never told anyone this except you. I'm on my own now, and when I'm in bed and you dream about this, that and the other, I don't dream about being made love to. I dream about getting used. Just being used, cause I feel that's all that's ever happened in my life.

Children as mediators

As well as protecting warring partners against each other, children also tried to mediate between them. A mother described how her young Primary son had taken her hands and his father's and joined them together, expressing in this striking symbolic way his wish for them to reconcile. A young woman recalled that her goal in life always been to solve her parents' problems and stop them fighting - 'A marriage guidance counsellor at the age of seven'.

Sometimes the mediating role was not taken on at the child's initiative. The non-drinking mother of a Primary girl told how she used her to negotiate with her drinking father, because she was his favoured child and often the only one who could deal with him when he was drunk.

Children as confidants

Where conflict between parents was particularly acute and permanent, children indicated that they were sometimes drawn almost into a partnership with a parent who turned to them for company, advice and emotional support. Hence, one young woman spent most of her time at home rather than go out with friends, as she knew her mother (the non-drinker) had no other company.

An even more striking example was of an oldest child used as ally and confidant by both her drinking father and her non-drinking mother. The torn loyalties involved had been very stressful and according to her parents may have contributed to the fact that she later developed anorexia:

> *Mother* - I know as an alcoholic parent - and on my side as well, we both used Betty. You know, discussed things wi' her - things that shouldnae have been in a way discussed with a girl of twelve, eleven, you know?
> *Interviewer* - What sort of things?
> *Mother* - Mair or less sort of confidential. The way I would talk about (her Dad) and his drinking and saying to her 'What d'ye think I should dae?' Whereas, I should have been able to make that decision for mysel', and I couldnae.
> *Father* - I could identify wi' that. Betty became my wife, if you like. You know, the person I went tae and shared my problems wi' an' ask her advice on things.

Alliances

The case described above was extreme, but other parents and children illustrated how families with drinking problems can split into opposing camps with children allied to one or other of the parents. Such divisions are not confined to families like these, of course.

A young adult described her parents, as involved in a game of 'sides', competing for the children's loyalty. Usually she allied herself with her mother, whereas her brother and sister allied with their father. In this case, both parents were drinkers. Where only one parent drank, children in our sample usually allied with the non-drinking parent. This brought benefits like protection or a sense of justification, but could also involve costs. Children sometimes had to act as informers, monitoring the drinking parent's consumption and noting tell-tale signs. Serious consequences could arise. In one family, the mother and both children were allied against the drinking father, but the mother was not able to protect the children adequately. Their alliance with her therefore left them vulnerable to psychological abuse by the father in his attempts to hurt her:

> *Mother* - The things he said to them were awful.
> *Interviewer* - Did you try to intervene?
> *Mother* - Oh yes, and I think that's why he did it. Because he would try and get me and I wouldn't rise to his bait. I had learned not to rise to the bait. And then he would start on Hazel, he knew that I wouldn't stand for it and I think that's why he did it. And I started thinking about it and that why he's doing it is to get at me. So if I say nothing, is he going to stop hassling her, because he's not getting the reaction he's wanting? But if I do nothing, she's going to think 'Mum doesn't even care'.

Not all children allied with the non-drinker, however. In one family, the three younger children supported their drinking father against their mother. The father explained this was because he was seen as the 'softer' parent, largely because his drinking led him to opt out of the 'control' aspect of the parental role. Only the eldest son took his mother's side.

According to his mother, one Primary boy identified very strongly with his drinking father, now away from home. This had led to serious family disagreements and tensions. The boy visited his father regularly on his own and, when quizzed by his mother, concealed the fact that his father had been drinking. She expressed anxiety about her son's impudence and aggression towards her over the past two years, which she believed was a result of him using his father as a role model. She was desperate for help:

> I still don't know if Sam, as I said to you earlier, if Sam is totally blind to his Dad's faults or he's just ignoring them. As soon as I open my mouth to Sam he thinks I'm bringing his Dad down to him and he's on the defensive right away. So I canny really sit and talk to him like that. Cos' if I do it, it's me that's Big Bad Mum, I'm causing trouble, d'ye know what I mean?

The boy himself indicated that he saw both the 'good' and the 'bad' in his father. He described his anger and distress at the violence, yet added that his father still loved him. This family illustrates how problems can persist and even intensify for children after the drinker has left the household. It also illustrates the importance of obtaining multiple perspectives on the same set of relationships.

Circular patterns of causality and the attribution of blame

Most of the parents and children in the sample were clear about the direction of causation, namely that the parents drank (for their own reasons) and the children suffered. However, in a few families, at least in some circumstances, the direction of impact was seen as reversed or at least as circular. Two lone mothers specifically said they drank because of the behaviour of their children. One said her children totally ignored her and took her for granted both as a parent and an individual, She only felt able to assert herself when she had a drink. Her daughter also portrayed the drinking as related to their 'cheekiness' and failure to help with housework.

The other mother also attributed her drinking to the pressures of being a single parent, especially having to cope with her son's poor school attendance and delinquency. The boy himself explained his mother's drinking partly in terms of his father's past violence towards her, but acknowledged that his own behaviour was sometimes responsible. He said that when he was in trouble, his mother drank and blamed him for it. The reciprocal effects were revealed when he stated later that he went out and got into trouble when he felt depressed about her drinking.

Another Secondary boy interpreted his mother's drinking and his own behaviour in terms of circular causality:

> *Interviewer* - Can you think of any reason why your Mum drinks?
> *Mark* - It's usually I think cause we've been bad.
> *Interviewer* - Right, it's cos you've been bad?
> *Mark* - Aha. But it makes me be bad because it's her that drinks. She drinks for a day then she drinks for the rest of the days.

His mother also acknowledged that her drink caused the children's problems, but that she then drank in response to them.

The idea that the child's response to parental drinking can then act as a trigger, or fuel to fire the flame was also expressed by one young adult. He felt with hindsight that his attempts to stop his father drinking had in fact made it worse:

> (I tried to make him stop) by telling him how much I hated him and how much I wanted him to stop drinking. I remember screaming at the top of my voice how much I hated him... I blamed him for everything that was bad... I think he must have thought 'Well, my family hates me so what else have I got?' so he looked for solace in the drink. I think to a certain extent, I feel a bit guilty that I done that, but obviously I was very young and did not know what I was doing.

These accounts are interesting, not just as examples of cyclical processes operating in the family system, but because they represent the few cases in the sample where children or young adults did express some responsibility themselves for their parents' behaviour. Even then this did not always take the form of straightforward references to self-blame. Feelings of pervasive guilt and responsibility for parental drinking feature largely in the psychotherapeutic literature on children of drinkers and also in publicity material produced for them (Velleman, 1993a; 1995). However this did not emerge as a major theme from our interviews with children. In general their attributions were more sophisticated, and less unidirectional. They recognised that adults have their own reasons for drinking in the first place, but that sometimes their reactions may then exacerbate rather than help the situation. Similarly a young adult was clear that his parents were responsible for the drinking, but that his behaviour then fed into a destructive process:

Interviewer - (following up a denial of any current sense of blame) But did a bit of you feel to blame at the time, even though you don't think that now?
Young adult - At times. Getting them worried, things like that, what's going to happen to me, the glue sniffing. I think maybe a wee bit, I blamed myself. But no very much. I blame them for me getting into it, for me running away and that, cos if they never drank as much as they did, I would have stopped in the house. I would have had a better education. Because I was never at school.

Also contrary to stereotype, some parents expressed intense guilt at what their drinking had done to their children. For instance:

Interviewer - What effect do you think the drinking's had on Donna?
Father - (struggling with emotion throughout) I'd say it's held Donna back quite a lot. (Long pause) I'd do everything completely different. Donna worries me greatly. (Long pause) In a way I've destroyed her.

Loss of parental authority

A striking feature of many of the sample families was lack of respect for the drinking parent, which in some cases was explicitly linked to the drinking. A number of factors contributed to this. First, drinking often led to parental laxity or inattention, with children 'allowed to run riot'. As one young woman said disapprovingly: 'Raymond, my wee brother just thought he could do whatever he wanted just because of the drinking and that'. Once children had become used to freedom, it could then be hard for the parent to reassert authority when sober.

Secondly, the experience of seeing a parent behaving 'stupidly', out of control or immaturely can undermine any sense that they have a right to tell you what to do:

> *Mother* - As they were growing up they would think 'Oof, I'm not going to listen to that, he drinks, how can he tell us what to do?' you know?. When (his Dad) was making a perfectly reasonable request (to a teenage boy), he wasn't asking him to do anything outrageous, he was asking him to behave in a reasonable manner and he would say to me, 'Why would I listen to that old drunk?' so you know, lack of respect.

Thirdly, when a parent has behaved in a way which is socially unacceptable, it provides the child with potent psychological ammunition with which to defend themselves against a similar charge. For example, one father found his young son's acting out hard to deal with, since when told 'don't do that' the boy retorted: 'Well, you broke the lamp!' This evoked in the father feelings that it was his fault his son's behaviour was difficult, so undermining his ability to deal with him firmly.

In several families, the parent-child boundary seemed to have largely broken down. We observed parents and children engaging in name-calling and taunts about each other's handwriting, more like peers than members of different generations. In one family, a Primary boy appeared to be out of his lone mother's control, totally ignoring her orders, threats and cajoing. At one point he told her 'You're crap'. In another family, two young adults spoke of their father as if he were a delinquent adolescent whose antics they disapproved of but tolerated.

An attitude of dismissive contempt developed in some cases. A young adult spoke approvingly of how another child dealt with a drunken father: 'She just walked in the door and if her Dad was lying in the hall, she give him a quick boot and things, but she never let it bother her'.

In other households, intergenerational authority had reversed, with the child as disapproving parent and the parent acting like a guilty child. The mother of a young boy described trying unsuccessfully to hide the evidence of her drinking from him:

> *Mother* - He used to see empty cans and he says to me (reproachfully) 'Have you been drinking beer?' I says 'No'. (copies her son's narky voice) 'Aye, there's the beer cans.' I tried to kid on they're my brother's.
> *Interviewer* - Did he believe you?
> *Mother* - No.

Another striking example of such reversal was shown by one Secondary girl. She was normally quiet and retiring, but her mother and father described how, when they were both drinking, she became very assertive and acted in many ways like a parent to them. She refused to go out and leave them unchaperoned, physically tried to chastise her father and reproached both of them for their poor behaviour and failure to keep promises. This was vividly described by her mother:

> She would smack him and shout and bawl at him, you know and just 'See you!' and call him everything under the sun. And that's when you see the other side of her - if she gives you a shirriking, you just take it!

These two parents portrayed how they acted like guilty school children, trying to get away with a misdemeanour:

> When Jim (father) was there and he used to say (sotto voce) 'D'ye want a drink?' Then I'd go roon to the off-licence and then (mime of guilty whispers) you're sneaking in the door an' trying no' to look at Ann's face. It's a horrible feeling! ...You're frightened to look at her face and you're talking to her to see if she's still - but Jim was always good at that, he would get her roon to something funny.

Finally, one young woman recalled taking action for the sake of her drunken father and herself which might inadvertantly have proved harmful:

> But it was comical the things I used to dae but it was kinda dangerous because when I put him to bed I'd bang his head against the wall to make sure he was sleeping all night. I mean this is the sort of things you'd dae just to get peace - peace of mind, to get a good night's sleep.

Shutting off the outside world

It has been widely suggested that families affected by heavy drinking tend to set up barriers to conceal the drinking from the outside world. This defensive instinct usually originates with one or both parents, but the children may also feel under pressure to avoid or minimise contacts which might bring the drinking and its shameful associations to the attention of outsiders. Perhaps with differing motivations, drinkers, their partners and the children may collude in a conspiracy of silence about the problem.

Our sample of parents and children by definition excluded families who were successful in concealing the drinking altogether or who, although in touch with an agency, were not prepared to speak about it to researchers. Nevertheless, the families varied considerably in the extent to which outsiders were allowed to know about the drinking problem. Only a few appeared to be completely open, and they either lived in areas where their drinking was the norm or had come from such a background themselves. The remainder had either been secretive in the past, or still were.

Some children had been coached from an early age 'not to tell', with clearly defined categories of people who could and could not be confided in. In certain families, they would be allowed to confide in grandparents, but not anyone else. In other cases grandparents were precisely those who must on no account know. Children could be quick to recognise the need for discretion:

> *Mother* - When you're drinking and you're saying to them 'Remember don't say your Mum was drunk last night.' So I think they're really watching what they're saying and it's in the back of their minds. I mean, I'll even say to David 'You didnae say to (neighbour) that 'Mummy was drunk last night?' He goes 'No.' (Tone of voice indicates 'As if I would')

Parents confirmed that in some cases it was unnecessary to give explicit prohibitions - the children simply absorbed the message as part of family culture:

> *Mother* - I think that was mair or less ma job, if you want to put it that way. We never included the children into that. (pause) I don't think I had to say to them, I think they knew within theirsel' no' to say nothing. I canny remember saying to them 'Don't dae this and don't dae that.' They just knew, you know.

Children also admitted to being guarded with outsiders, because of the shame associated with drinking problems. In such cases, secrecy could result more from concern about reactions by peers than explicit or implicit parental injunctions:

> It has been quite hard because some of my friends talk about like they wouldn't like their Dad to be an alcoholic and I've always wanted to tell one of them about my Dad being an alcoholic. But I just find it dead hard to keep it inside me but I feel it's something I want to keep within ma family.

However, for some children, it was part of a general ethos of keeping all family matters private, as several of the young adults confirmed.

One young woman said she was brought up with the notion that 'our business is our business'.

Some families have a suspicion of professionals or a fear of 'the authorities'. One young adult said his parents had instilled in him an 'anti social worker' feeling, so he saw them as threatening rather than as possible confidants. Even one Secondary boy who had a good relationship with his social worker said he didn't talk to him openly, but only offered him snippets of information and sometimes left the house because he didn't feel like talking.

Thus, even within this group of families who had consented to talk with researchers, there was quite a degree of secrecy from outsiders and selectivity about who should know about the drinking. This restricted some families' social contacts. Two children said they were discouraged by their mother from having friends home, in case their father would be seen drinking, so they soon stopped asking. Two others explained that they no longer had other children to stay after friends witnessed their father assaulting their mother. Two young adults also said they had felt unable to bring friends home because of their fathers' drunkenness.

Velleman (1995) observed from his retrospective study that the offspring of heavy drinkers tend either to be socially isolated or have strong peer relationships which are kept separate from the family of origin. Similarly several of the children from our study in families with closed communication about the drinking nevertheless had good friends whom they saw both at school and outside. Social isolation was only a problem for a handful of children in the sample and even then was not necessarily linked to the drinking.

Summary

Problem drinking often affected the allocation of social and emotional roles within families so that children took on responsibilities which are normally held by adults. In many families some degree of role-reversal took place, with children physically caring for parents in minor ways when they were drunk, protecting the non-drinking parent from violence (sometimes at the parent's request), mediating between the parents during conflicts and negotiating with one partner on behalf of the other. Children were also used as confidants by their parents, sometimes assuming an almost spouse-like role. We should remember, though, that there are wide variations in child-adult relationships amongst families in general and there are other contexts (like bereavement) when children may seek to protect parents emotionally or socially.

A number of children in the sample formed alliances with or against the drinking parent. This led to tensions with the other partner.

Children's behaviour was sometimes reported to have triggered or exacerbated drinking episodes, but in general children did not express guilt nor say they blamed themselves for parental drinking. In many families there was a loss of respect for the drinker, with children regarding themselves as authority figures in relation to the drinking. As expected, families were often secretive about the drinking problem, but in only a few cases did this result in social isolation for the children.

6. Coping, support and communication

In this chapter we consider the ways in which children attempted to cope with parental problem drinking and the factors which helped them to do so. We examine first the influence of individual or family characteristics, then proceed to more active coping mechanisms, the importance of support from other people and the significance of communication.

Child and family characteristics which were thought to affect impact

The study was based on one-off contacts with a small sample and was not designed to assess the precise relationship between particular characteristics and coping processes or outcomes. However, respondents themselves often explained differences in terms of personal or situational characteristics, so their views will be reported, supplemented by indications from comparing differences within the sample. Interestingly, nobody raised the child's gender as a factor, but gender differences did emerge from our comparisons, which will be noted later in this chapter.

Age and stage

All societies are organised in some way into groups distinguished by age (LaFontaine, 1986). It has also been a truism of developmental psychology that children progress through distinct stages which occur at similar ages for all or most children (LeFrancois, 1990). Yet it is easy to over emphasise the differences related to age, ignore the wide variations which can occur at the same age and devalue both the awareness and capacities of younger children (James and Prout, 1990; Mayall, 1994).

Parents, children and young adults in the study all considered that the nature of the impact of problem drinking on a child varied with age. One or two teenagers thought that younger children suffered more. For instance it was suggested they felt puzzled or guilty when parents shouted, believing this was due to their own misbehaviour and not realising it resulted from drinking. However, most parents and older children believed that the impact was less on younger children. They felt that younger children were largely protected from distress by their ignorance and innocence. Either they were oblivious to what was going on or they simply regarded heavy drinking as normal parental behaviour. There was considerable consensus about the age when children start seeing their parent's drinking as abnormal. Most parents and young adults said this awareness occurred between eight and ten. Significantly, however, the youngest children in the sample were well able to link behaviour changes to alcohol consumption and to verbalise the discrepancy between their parents' drinking pattern and that of other adults. So age may shelter children less than many adults assume.

Personality

It is recognised that some children are by nature very sensitive to trauma, while others appear remarkably stress-resistant (Garmezy, 1985). Rutter (1985) observed that 'even with the most severe stressors and the most glaring adversities, it is unusual for more than half of children to succumb' (p. 598). A number of factors have been identified which appear to contribute to resilience. Some are external, such as educational opportunities and supportive adults, but others are internal, such as temperament and self-esteem (Werner, 1986; Antonovsky, 1987). Most probably these factors interact. For instance a confident child may be more able to build up supportive relationships which in turn may reinforce a positive self-image.

Our direct contacts, though brief, together with parental accounts, suggested this was true of children in our sample. Some seemed to take a degree of problem drinking in their stride, whereas others suffered badly. A Primary child was described by her older sister as: 'A tough wee cookie, so she is. She can look after herself'. One young adult had been very upset by parental drinking, according to her parents and herself. Her young brother, however, was said to regard it with amusement and to have had no problems coping, although he was not interviewed and may or may not have confirmed this view himself. He was said to speak out plainly when disturbed by arguments: 'You two are keeping me awake'. He also demanded attention when he needed it and joined in the fun when his parents were merry.

In addition to these two children, our sample contained at least six others across the age span who did not appear to be deeply troubled by parental drinking, although all disliked it. Both direct encounters and parental reports indicated that they were gregarious individuals with outside interests, which may in part have accounted for their more robust responses to the drinking. As one mother said, comparing her teenage daughter with the rest of the family:

I really don't think it's such a terrible problem for Audrey because she's the type that's in quite a lot of things. You know, she's got too much to sit and worry about her father, sort of thing.

It may be relevant that all of these apparently more resilient children had older siblings, which brings us on to the question of birth order.

Birth order

When parents note significant differences in their children, they frequently explain these in terms of birth order, as well as age and gender (Hill, 1987). In fact, extensive quantitative research has failed to reveal large systematic effects of birth order on personality, which is not surprising when we consider the complex way in which position in the family is affected by age gaps, the gender of self and siblings and differential life experiences, as well as the interplay between parent-child and child-child interaction (Sutton-Smith and Rosenberg, 1970; Ernst and Angst, 1983). Nevertheless, there is little doubt that birth order does affect the processes of growing up, but its significance and impact will depend on the specific family context (Dunn and McGuire, 1992).

There were a number of examples given of first borns seeking to protect younger brothers or sisters. In one large family, a pair of twins were thought by the parents to have been particularly unaffected by the drinking because each had a different older sister to look after them. In several cases parent-child aggression seemed to focus on the eldest child still at home. Two young siblings said their father's violence was mainly directed at their eldest sister who was singled out by virtue of being the oldest as 'the one who should get the doings'. One young adult described how his elder brother had protected him when his drunken father was wielding a knife, whilst another who was the eldest child in the family thought his younger brother had been picked on less because he could shelter behind himself.

Whereas an older child may feel the brunt of responsibility for challenging a drunken parent or shielding a sibling, so younger children within a household may correspondingly feel less entitled to express their views. A Secondary girl who was the youngest of four said:

> I always wanted to say something to him but I didn't feel it was my place and I wouldn't really want to because I'm the youngest and I didn't feel it was my place.

The social context of drinking

A further factor which may modify impact or help children to cope is the perceived acceptability of heavy drinking in their particular environment (neighbourhood or extended family). We have already discussed how families in heavy drinking cultures may see very heavy drinking as normal and acceptable. Where this was the case, it seemed to be another factor which eased the strain for children, who regarded their parents as acting appropriately within their social circle. The following quote is interesting because it indicates the influence of the child's milieu in normalising heavy drinking even in the face of majority standards:

> I remember once in school we were asked in Religious Education whose parents drank and three quarters of the class put their hands up. Whose parents drink at Christmas and New Year, half the class put their hands up. Whose parents drink every weekend, it got smaller. Whose parents drink every day? And I remember there was two of us put our hands up in the class and my Mum and her Mum were friends. Not best friends but we had quite similar lifestyles. And I remember thinking, "Wow! You lot are abnormal". Not "Wow! our parents are abnormal". And I thought oh it's just the school I'm at and people don't live the way we live. But I was more put off by the fact that everybody's parents didn't drink than that mine did and it didn't make me question the fact that mine did.

Personal coping responses

We have seen that some children were helped or hindered in coping by virtue of factors which were largely outside their control, such as their temperament, position in the family or drinking norms in the local context. But many children also made proactive efforts to deal with parental drinking. These took two main forms:

- trying to tackle the drinking problem itself

- handling the emotions aroused by it.

Problem-focused coping

Most of the children had made some attempt to stop the drinking, whether by giving feedback or by active intervention to deny their parents access to alcohol. A few children monitored parental drinking, either in combination with to efforts to stop it or as an alternative. A young Primary child kept an eye open for beer cans and challenged his mother when he saw them. Several other children also regularly sought to assess their parents drinking, perhaps by noting the contents of shopping bags or marking bottles to measure consumption. They hoped that parents' awareness that they were being observed and that the amount they drank was being measured might inhibit them from drinking.

Many children had also taken more direct action to try and prevent their parents drinking, either by asking them to stop or by restricting their access to alcohol. Hence a young adult described her attempts:

> Talking to them and that and telling them I was fed up with watching yous ... drinking all the time and fighting and that. (Saying) 'I've just had enough - I'm fed up wi' it'.

A young Primary boy tried to obstruct purchase of alcohol.

> *Interviewer* - Does Mark ever try to stop you drinking?
> *Mother* - He doesnae like me going to the wholesalers. I was in there last night for cigarettes. 'Don't go in there, don't go in there Mammy!' I just went in for cigarettes and he got a sweetie and that was him quite happy then.
> *Interviewer* - But he worried you might get some cans?
> *Mother* (nods)

One child watered down the contents of a vodka bottle to reduce its effects. A Primary girl who appeared to accept a fair degree of heavy drinking as normal, took decisive action when she thought it had gone on too long:

> If it's like one night then a night and then a morning I've did it. I've poured the vodka down the sink at my Aunt Mary's and I've poured the beer and all that down the sink and I've always said it was my Aunty Lilian cause she doesn't know what she does anymore. My Aunt Lilian hallucinates.

It was clear that many children did not see themselves as passive victims of parental drinking, but as instrumental agents capable of taking action to prevent or mitigate it - however ineffective that might turn out to be. However others developed feelings of helplessness after a while. One Secondary boy said it was no use trying to stop his Mum from drinking because she had said 'she's gonnae drink until she dies'. Yet when asked to make three wishes, his second choice (after playing for his local football team) was for 'My Ma to come off the drink'.

Emotion-focused coping

Since their efforts to influence the amount of parental drinking was usually unsuccessful, most of the children recognised their limitations and concentrated on coping with the emotional impact of drinking on themselves. They did this in various ways.

Avoidance The most common response was to keep out of the way. Many children retreated to their rooms to keep away from the sight of the drinking and resultant behaviour, although they could usually still hear the arguments and other associated noises. One young woman said she used to: 'Just shut the door and things and try and not hear 'em and that. But it was hard to do that'.

A pair of Secondary girls retreated to their bedroom, sometimes joined by their mother, and locked the door. Retreat was not always successful, however, because some parents resented avoidance and went in pursuit, as one young man explained:

> I tried to stay in my room a lot... But sometimes they would still come in my room. My stepma she would start shouting at us. Then that would start my Da'. Then my Da' would start on us. There wasn't much you could have done about it, you know what I mean?

As a result, he started leaving the house, a tactic also adopted by several of the other males in the sample. A Secondary boy explained:

> *Child* - I just stay oot all night. I just walk about the streets
> *Interviewer* - how does that make you feel?
> *Child* - Terrible

A young adult recalled doing this even when under 7 - the age at which his father had stopped drinking:

> I can remember it all you know what I'm saying. (Pause) Like wi' me being young, I'd maybe see a big fight, I could go away oot and play football or something you know? ... forget aboot it and gae and do something wi' ma pals. But when I came back it was always going to be there.

Keeping watch In contrast to the boy just referred to, none of the females reported leaving house on their own as a coping strategy. Although one young woman had done so, it was in the company of her mother and other children and they normally ended up staying with extended family. In contrast, some girls tended to go to the opposite extreme, keeping watch on the drinker and the precarious family situation. Although, a desire to protect the non-drinking parent doubtless played a part in this, the main motivation seemed to be a need to know what was going on. Hence one young woman said:

> I wouldn't leave the house if they were fighting, not because I was frightened of what would happen to them, but because I was

frightened of what would happen. It's almost as if 'If I'm not here, I won't know what's going on'.

Another young woman explained that after a regular Wednesday drinking session by her father she normally did not attend school the next day because she was frightened in case anything went wrong at home. A young man told us that while he used to flee the house when his father was drinking, his sisters made a point of staying close by when there was a fight. According to their mother, they did this not in order to intervene, but so that they would at least know what had happened. For all these children, full knowledge was preferred to uncertainty or avoidance.

Although in our sample keeping watch was a common female strategy, it is clearly also sometimes used by boys. The children in the Support Group, which included both boys and girls, put 'worrying about parents' at the top of their list of problems. They too said they did not like being long away from home in case something happened to their parents.

Externalisation Another common coping strategy for dealing with the emotional reaction to drinking was to externalise it by focusing energy on other activities. Here again, we came across clear gender differences in our sample.

Several of the boys tended to 'act out' their feelings of anger and frustration in anti-social ways. A Primary boy engaged in verbal retaliation towards his mother and seemed to gain considerable satisfaction from defying her and showing he was in control. Two Secondary boys from different families both linked their law-breaking activities to their reactions to their mothers' drinking:

> *Boy* - sometimes it just depresses me and I gae oot and I'm really depressed. I go and do something - get caught. Some other times I just ignore her.
>
> *Interviewer* - Could you say in what way it's affected you all?
> *Boy* - It's just started me being bad and all that and getting tempers and stealing motors.

It is worth noting that none of the males in the sample, of whatever age, had liked school. Some hated it, and several were non-attenders.

By contrast, with one exception, the females in our sample appeared more likely to channel their frustrations into productive or pro-social behaviour. Only two admitted they had gone through a rebellious period at school, but said the effects of this were short-lived. Most of the girls said they enjoyed school and had good relationships with at least some teachers. Several seemed to be doing extremely well both in school and in extra-curricular activities. While this might be related to ability, it was suggested to us by both parents and children that this might also be a way of coping:

> The school had absolutely no idea that there was any problem at home at all. Their school work was excellent, their reports were superb. At parents' evenings there were glowing reports on both of them. Only one teacher noticed that Heather was a bit nervy. It was suggested to me that this was their way of escape, that they channelled all their energies into their school work and they would forget what was happening at home..... It sounds quite reasonable.

A longitudinal study of young women who had been brought up in care also found that positive school experiences were associated with more satisfactory functioning in adulthood (Quinton and Rutter, 1988).

Interestingly, a Secondary girl mentioned coping with noisy nights in a way many parents would warm to:

> My room is straight above the living room and so I can hear everything he says. You can't get to sleep or anything so I just get up in the middle of the night and tidy my bedroom (laughs).

Another young woman also highlighted gender differences:

> I think as children the way we reacted to them affected the way we felt and the way we are now. We all coped differently, the way we behaved. I coped by believing everything my mother said was right and my mother was mine and my Mum said my Dad was bad: my Dad was bad. My brother coped by rebelling, I think, but he might have rebelled anyway, he was a rebellious child ... My sister just kept herself to herself and studied incessantly and did very well for herself.

The gender differences apparent in our sample fit with evidence from the wider literature that more males than females cope poorly with family relationship difficulties, although there is much overlap and this may simply reflect more overt responses by boys (Nicholson, 1984; Schaffer, 1990). Also, in general, females are more willing and able to recognise, express and deal with deeper emotions (Duncombe and Marsden, 1995). Nevertheless, caution is needed in interpreting our data about the influence of gender on coping reactions to problem drinking. The differences may have been due to social background factors and sample bias. More females than males agreed to take part in the study and they came from a variety of social backgrounds, including a few with professional parents. In contrast, none of our males were from middle class homes and all but one of the boys under 17 were living with unemployed lone parents. Thus poverty may have been as important as gender. Several of the more affluent families in the sample also had boys who were doing well at school, with high aspirations for the future, but who did not wish to be interviewed.

Internalisation The children above were able to cope with their anger and anxiety by directing them into outside activities and this seemed to be the majority response in our sample. However, a few children appeared to cope with emotional conflict differently by internalising their feelings of anger and frustration. For example one young woman used to redirect feelings of anger and blame about her parent's drinking onto herself, as her father painfully described:

> *Father* - No matter what I would say, she couldnae stop it. And she would go to her bed crying, she'd be angry. But that still didnae stop it. We still drank.
> *Interviewer* - She was upset?
> *Father* - Oh, very. She would voice her opinions, but it was falling on deaf ears. And she would - the terrible thing aboot it was - she would voice her opinions, she'd be angry an' then she'd go away crying, she'd go to her bedroom. And then she'd come doon when we'd started drinking, say maybe about an hour, and apologise tae us. She would apologise tae us because she thought that she was upsetting us. She actually turned it roon in her ain heid an' blamed hersel' for what she says. An yet we knew it's us.

The interview with the young woman herself indicated that she was quite home-centred and isolated from her peers. Latterly she had gained more confidence to challenge her parents and express her anger towards them both verbally and physically.

Supports

Up to now we have looked at the children's individual coping efforts. However, most also gained support from other people. Some had a great deal. This support came both from within the family (in its widest sense) and from outsiders. Some of the children had also received professional help, which we consider in Chapter 7.

Children were asked about support they received in general and also more specifically about who was their main confidant. Nearly always that role was taken by a close family member, usually female. Mothers were the most common confidant, followed by grandmothers, aunts, uncles and siblings. Fewer children confided primarily in their father, or in a friend. This patterns accords with other findings about support and confiding (Youniss and Smollar, 1985). One child named a professional as a main confidant. Only two children had no confidant at all.

Intra-familial support

Parents The first and most obvious source of support for many children would be their parents. About half the children in the sample were living with or in close touch with a non-drinking parent. At a basic level, these parents were all apparently able to keep a structure of normal life going for their children - cooking, cleaning, keeping to some sort of routine, making sure they got to school. They also managed to keep the family afloat financially, despite difficulties. This was very important to children and much appreciated in retrospect, as these young adults pointed out:

> I was really lucky because I had ma Ma. ... She would make sure we were all right - clothes and all that and food - food on the table and that sort of thing.

> I went on a trip to Germany and I honestly don't know how my Mum could have afforded it, but I think there again obviously she probably thought that sending me away would probably help, maybe ease the pressure in the house.

Although none of the non-drinking parents in our sample had kept the drinking secret from their children, some were able to reassure them about it and convey to the child that they were in charge. As one young man explained:

> If there was an argument and me and my brother got out of bed, she would always tell us to go back to bed and not to worry, that everything was OK, you know, that she would sort it out, so she did protect us very, very well, I would say. As much as she could. I mean obviously there was things that happened that she couldn't protect us from, but you know she was always there, trying to help.

Some non drinking parents helped their children by tackling the drinking directly; seeking help for the drinker or pressurising them into seeking it themselves. In extreme situations, they were able to protect children by removing them from the house, calling the police or effecting a separation.

The non-drinking parent could also offer support and advice to the child about coping with the drinker. This provided practical help and gave a sense of responsibility shared. Hence one Secondary boy's father explained how to cope with his mother's shakes:

> *Child* - When I got older ma Da' told us about what drink did to you. It gives you fits and all that. Ma Da' was telling us so I just got used to it from there. Ma Da' has had to put up with everything.
> *Interviewer* - Did you find that helpful?
> *Child* - If you see how they shake and all that you just go in and get her a can cause she gets up sometimes and she canna walk she's that bad. (Voice quavers slightly)
> *Interviewer* - So you think it's helpful to know what to do?
> *Child* - If they're in that state, aye.

Some non-drinking parents also gave their children emotional support. Several children said that they were very close to their (non drinking) mothers and confided in them, although this happened less often than might have been expected, as we shall see later when discussing communication.

The drinking parent could also be seen as a source of support. This usually involved binge drinkers during the intervals between bouts, when the relationships with the child could be a warm one. In two cases, the (drinking) father was the one who left the house when the couple separated, so that the children could have the stability of remaining at home. Both these fathers remained in close contact with their children throughout the separation. A mother in a different family who had a severe drinking problem was very close to her daughters and remained in contact after the separation. The girls told us they could 'tell her anything'. And even when both parents were drinkers, they could sometimes create a positive environment for the child. Two young Primary children seemed to have caring relationships with each of their parents who both drank heavily. These parents took an active interest in their education. One young woman said that she received a great deal of affection from her parents, had a rich social life and a good education. In neither of these two families, however, were the parental drinking problems viewed as particularly obtrusive by the children.

Finally, some families appeared to support children in developing their lives outside the home, especially at school. Success in outside activities could compensate for the problems at home.

Siblings Brothers and sisters are popularly believed to be a significant support in times of stress, although there is also potential for intensified rivalry and unhelpful dependency relationships (Hegar, 1988; Kosonen, 1994). Our sample likewise provided examples of close support, but also instances where each child in the family seemed to deal with the drinking in their own way and on their own. This may not affect the eventual outcome for each child, but sharing problems is likely to bring relief and reduce the risks of self-blame.

About half of the children with siblings mentioned helping or being helped by them. A few older sisters looked after much younger children, sometimes adopting a quasi-maternal role. There were examples of siblings:

- substituting for parents (e.g. cooking a meal for them)

- seeking external help in a crisis (e.g. getting a young child dressed and taking him to his Gran's when his mother was drinking)

- offering comfort and companionship.

One young woman offered her young Primary sister sanctuary in her room: 'Some other times she just comes upstairs into ma bedroom and just sits with me (pause) - listen to tapes or whatever - trying to ignore all the things that happen downstairs'.

It might be expected that siblings would also offer each other emotional support through mutual confiding, but in fact only two made mention of this. One Secondary girl talked to her elder brother, to whom she felt very close. A trio of sisters said that they had warm and open relationships with each other. The youngest child confided in the eldest, whilst the two older girls gave each other mutual support:

Interviewer - What's helped you cope?
Young person - Each other really. We're not close - we're not loving sisters (both laugh) but if one's in trouble, the other one helps. We've really just stuck by each other and helped each other. I kept in touch with Fiona when she moved to another Home. We've always kept in contact. We have been there for each other.

Otherwise references to siblings suggested that they normally made only brief and superficial allusions to the drinking, e.g. 'He's had a bit too much tonight'. One young man recalled:

My brother and I spoke about it, but the only way we spoke about it was how we could get my father out, so that would have been the only way it was spoke about.

Although discussions and speculations about the drink might not lead to any direct action, they could help children develop their own thinking and coping strategies in relation to the drink:

Interviewer - Do you talk to your sister about your Mum's drinking?
Child - Diane will say 'She's a right wee pain aint she?' I'd say 'Aye - it's just 'cause o' the drink.' Then me and Diane start talking 'Do

you think ma ma will go into another place so she can get aff the drink?'

In the rest of the families, siblings did not seem to communicate about the drinking at all. One young adult, a youngest boy with four older sisters, said he never talked about his father's drinking to them and did not find them supportive.

Extended Family   Support from other relatives was frequently reported, with grandparents being by far the most common confidants and helpers. In two families, the maternal grandmother occasionally provided substitute care for younger children when the mother was drinking. In another three families, the maternal grandparents had been a refuge for both mothers and children during the fathers' violent outbursts.

Grandparents also afforded emotional support. Several other children mentioned their grandmother as a principal confidant or as a favourite person, for example this young Primary child:

Interviewer - Is there anybody you can talk to when you feel upset and worried?
Child - No.
Interviewer - Do you just keep it to yourself?
Child - I keep to me and ma Gran.

Sometimes grandparents were able to offer advice as well as support, based on their own experience of problem drinking:

She's experienced it herself - getting shouted at by my Mum. She understands what I'm going through because she's been through it all.

In another family, where the father's drinking had effectively excluded him from normal family life, we were told by the young adult concerned that as a child he often spent weekends with his grandparents, appreciating the peace and quiet there in contrast to his parental home. He described his maternal grandfather as acting like a father figure to the children. For example he took the children out on day trips which their parents never did.

Aunts, uncles and cousins were also mentioned a few times as sources of support. One aunt had a young child to stay when his lone mother was in a Detox unit. In another instance, a secret code was used to call an uncle for help when the father was violent:

So if he did anything, Mum only had to phone up Uncle Richard and say 'Not bad' and he'd be down straight away (laughs).

It is clear then that extended family members play a significant part in helping children cope with problem drinking, but as one case showed, there could be limits to this:

> We were up through the night walkin' the streets and... and we'd been to every relation we'd had. Basically they were sick o' it... for years and years we'd been going to their doors through the night and nothing was changing. She was gonnae leave and folk get sick o' hearing that.

Indeed one grandmother was a source of strain, not support. She was a strict teetotaller and lived in a Granny Flat in the family home. This created considerable difficulty for her daughter (the non-drinking partner), who felt obliged to conceal her husband's problem drinking from her mother.

Support from outside the family As well as turning to relatives, some children also turned to outsiders for support, usually friends of their own age. Their ability to do so depended partly on the family's attitude to talking to outsiders about family problems. Hence, as we have seen, in families where a high value was placed on privacy, children felt unable to confide in friends about parental drinking problems. Others were too reticent to try, as one parent who had herself grown up in a drinking family pointed out:

> I'm a very private person and, see my Mum and Dad arguing and I was in the middle an' that - a lot of girls gaunny go 'Right' and spoken to their friends 'I'm fed up wi' this carry on' an' a, but I just couldn't do that, I just held it in to myself.

Some did not want their personal problems to intrude on everyday conversations with friends, as a young adult made clear:

> I don't talk to them (friends) about ma Mum and ma Dad fighting and drinking and what have you. I talk to them about different kind of things like what they watch on the telly and what kind of music they like and all that.

As the last quotation shows, friends can be a source of pleasure and support simply through their company, even when they are not party to innermost secrets. However, for other children, friends did additionally become major confidants. Some children seemed adept at locating others with similar problems, for mutual confiding and advice. A Primary child spoke of her friend, who was in a similar position to herself:

Child - Julie's Mum drinks a lot.
Interviewer - Do you and Julie talk about it?
Child - Julie always gets angry when her Mum drinks and gets cheeky. So when I stay with Julie I just tell her to sit down and calm down and go to sleep.

When friends did not share the same problem, it could be easier to confide when they already knew about it, so that the hurdle of when and how to bring up the subject did not arise. Hence, one young woman, though brought up not to speak to outsiders about family matters, was able to confide in a particular friend who had witnessed their family arguments. Similarly a Secondary girl talked about her father to one special friend, who had seen him drunk many times and appeared non-judgmental about it. Another young woman described how she was helped to cope by confiding in friends 'who saw everything that was happening'.

It seems clear that, perhaps particularly for girls, peers can offer a significant degree of support. Few children said they opened up to an adult non-relative. One confided in the father of her best friend and another in his guidance teacher and IT worker.

Spiritual support For a few of our respondents, especially older ones, spiritual beliefs and the associated membership of a community of fellow adherents offered support. One young adult emphasised how important this was for him. He had a heavy drinking father, for whom he retained strong feelings of anger and hatred into adulthood. He became a committed Christian in early adulthood (after his father's death) and felt it had transformed his life, giving it meaning and purpose. It also enabled him retrospectively to forgive his father and to turn his experience to positive use in work with young people through the Church. He said:

> If I wasn't a Christian I wouldn't be helping young people, I'd probably be in the pub... Being a Christian has really helped me. Now looking back, I would say I am a much stronger person for it happening.

Another adult, an eldest girl in a different family, was also reported by her parents to have been helped in this way. They said she had assumed much of the emotional burden of helping the whole family cope with her father's drinking. This was connected with the fact that, while she was still at school, she was a good friend of the local minister's daughter, was treated as one of their family and became a Christian.

Interestingly, we met other families who were regular churchgoers but who did not mention their beliefs at all as an aid to managing the drink-related problems. However, it seems for some people this is a significant and perhaps under-recognised source of strength in coping with trauma.

Communication

Communication and confiding are widely recognised as coping strategies in stressful situations, although some people prefer keeping matters to themselves. Research on topics as different as divorce, bereavement and adoption have shown that adults often communicate with children about these emotionally difficult matters in a cursorily inadequate way (Mitchell, 1985; Hill et al., 1989). Likewise we were struck by how limited communication seemed to be in the families in the study, particularly between parents and children, even though some of the parents believed it would be good for their children to talk to someone about their experiences.

Only two families appeared to have been totally open with their children about parental drinking. In some families parents and children said they had never talked about it. On two occasions it was apparent that children had not been told the purpose of our visit. Even where there had been some communication between parents and children, it was often partial (the talk was brief and about facts, not feelings) or one-way (the child told the parent what they thought of the drinking, but the parent did not respond, or the parent apologised for violent behaviour but did not allow the child to respond).

In some families, parents and children recognised this lack and explained it largely in terms of presumptions about children's cognitive or emotional immaturity. Sometimes younger children were believed not to know what was going on or else it was thought that talking would 'stir things up' for them. For this reason, we were twice allowed to talk to elder children, but not to their younger siblings. Another attribution which blocked communication was the belief that reminding children of traumatic events only upsets them. Two young Primary children said they had been very upset by the death of their cousin. Their mother had told them not to talk about it, though they told the interviewer they did, with each other, in bed at night. Adults might also not wish to discuss the drinking out of shame, and one parent acknowledged that this could block off opportunities for the child to say or ask what they wanted to:

> You don't want to talk about it the next day, you're so embarrassed - you're down, your hangover doesnae help. She was very emotional aboot it and you could see her looking at you, whenever I was released from the police station she'd be looking at me. I couldnae handle Lucy when it came to that situation. I would have tae ignore the situation completely. I would apologise 'I'm sorry aboot what

happened last night' but I'd make it as quick as possible so the embarrassment would be over and done wi', get the TV on, and get lost in maself. No give Lucy a chance to voice her opinions. And that must have been frustrating for her.

Reluctance to talk was not confined to drinking parents, since partners might feel unable to open up more issues they would then have to handle:

It's almost as if you're actually volunteering to take on another set of problems. Cause if you start talking to your children, you're going to have to accept their hurts as well. Which is hard to do as well. So not only are you taking on his problems, your problems, your hurt, his hurt, but all their hurt as well, you know? So it's really easier to shut it out and try - you know, I would hide it, deny it, I mean that must all be subconscious, it's not a conscious decision that, no, I'm not going to talk to them. You're definitely hurting very badly, you know, the one that isn't drinking, at least I did anyway and I still do.

Likewise, some children were reluctant to raise the subject, not wishing to add to the burden of the non-drinking parent:

Child 1 - Some things you can't say to Mum (Non-drinker). She's like... Mum and she's got to put up with it as well and that. And she knows what Dad used to be like so we can't really tell her what we think of him (subdued laughter). Sometimes I suppose because she's close to it and you just feel you can't talk to her sometimes. You'd think we'd be able to talk to her more cause she knows what it's like and that.
Interviewer - Are you close to you Mum?
Child 1 - Yes, but we can't talk to her about that.
Interviewer - I understand what you mean.
Child 2 - Cause she's got all the problems as well so it wouldn't be fair on her because she suffers from it all.
Child 1- As well.
Child 2 - When we're in bed and then if she got all our problems on top of that.

In view of the reticence about communicating within the family, many respondents identified a need for children to be able to talk to outsiders. Some parents felt it would be good for children to talk, but were unable to take this on themselves. Many of the children wanted to talk, but not to their parents. In practice, though, few had found it at all easy to confide in outsiders until they reached their late teens. Only then did it seem that the impulse to share the experience overrode the inhibiting factors. This has obvious service implications.

Styles of coping: influences and outcomes

We have seen a variety of coping strategies displayed by children in response to parental drinking. It is important to note that often the range of strategies open to a child can be limited by parents. As we have seen, open communication as a means of dealing with drink-related problems was frequently suppressed. One father sometimes refused to let his daughters go to their rooms to avoid his verbal violence and obliged them to stay put and listen:

> *Mother* - As I say, I would say to them you can go out, or you can go to your room, but if Dad said 'No, you sit there, and you stay there' they had to sit there and stay there. And that they found very difficult.
> *Interviewer* - And how did they cope with that?
> *Mother* - Well, they usually ended up in tears. (Mother herself near tears at this point.)

A Secondary girl told a similar story of parental restriction: 'When she's drinking she shouts at me a lot. I'd go to my Dad's but I know she wouldn't let me.'

On the other hand, family mores could foster positive coping strategies. Where value was placed on education and achievement, and activities outside the home were encouraged, this could enable children to escape from the stress of drinking by concentrating on those aspects of life.

It will be obvious that some attempts to cope with the feelings aroused by parental drinking may lead on to secondary problems. Boys who cope by shoplifting or wandering the streets at night create further difficulties for themselves and additional stresses for their parents which may in turn exacerbate the drinking problem. The extended family may offer support of a kind that may lead to future problems. The grandmother of one young child was his principal confidant and a source of emotional support, but also offered him 'secret' sips of wine. Some coping strategies seem more beneficial to children in the long run than others, a point we shall return to in the next chapter.

Summary

The adults and children interviewed held beliefs about the ways in which such factors as age, personality, birth order and social context influence the impact of problem drinking on children. In addition, children actively coped by means of a variety of responses. They tackled the drinking itself and dealt with the emotions it arouses by avoidance, externalisation (both positive and negative) and internalisation. There were suggestions of gender differences, with more females than males in our sample staying home during drunken episodes, internalising their anxieties and confiding in friends. External supports were important in helping children cope. These came from parents, siblings, extended family and friends. Only two children appeared to be dealing with the problems alone. Spiritual faith can also be a source of strength for some young people. Communication within the family was surprisingly little used as a way of coping, considering this sample was self selected by its willingness to talk about experiences. Coping style may be influenced by family norms, and may lead to positive or negative long term effects.

7 Longer term implications of parental problem drinking

The scope and time-scale of the study meant that it could not directly trace any longer term effects of drinking, but we are able to convey the views on this of some of the participants. In this we are inevitably drawing mainly on the views of the older Secondary children and young adults, together with those of their parents, supplemented by information from key professionals.

Negative effects

Educational failure

This was the most common theme, mentioned by several older children and young adults. Young people felt they had done less well at school because of parental drinking. Some of the effects were direct, such as a parent not getting up in the morning to take younger children to school or failure through alcohol-induced laxness to ensure that older children attended regularly. One young adult had regularly stayed off school to check up on the home situation after a session of violence. Several of the children had been before Children's Hearings for non-attendance. [In Scotland the Children's Hearings system deals with any child about whom there are concerns that compulsory measures of care may be needed, whether on account of inadequate care at home or the children's own behaviour (Martin et al., 1981). Hearings are less formal than family or youth courts.]

Other effects were indirect, such as when separations and frequent moves led to changes of school. Worry about events at home could result in poor concentration on school work. Some young adults spoke of a lack of parental interest, illustrated by the fact that nobody went up to the school on parent's nights. Most felt that their academic performance had been affected and that they had done less well than they might:

> I suppose it did affect that, because my Mum used to go out to her work in the morning when I got to fourth or fifth year, I couldn't

really be bothered going to school, so I used to lie in bed till eleven, but my father didn't try and get me to get up. He wasn't interested in sending me out to school where, if it had been my mother, she'd have got me by the ear and thrown me out.

Problem behaviour

Some young people had engaged in behaviour which caused problems to themselves or others, including breaking the law. It is not altogether surprising that they had experienced a combination of adverse factors - chronic drinking, violence and poverty.

Two of the Secondary children and one young adult felt parental drinking had caused them to engage in offending activities. The young people attributed this to the need to get out of the house and to cope with anger, so they ended up acting out in a socially unacceptable way. Parents, on the other hand, attributed it to their laxity and failure to supervise - letting the children 'run riot' when they were drunk. Other young people admitted to impulsiveness and mood swings, which they thought were either modelled on a drinking parent or developed in response to inconsistent parenting and drunken provocation. For example:

> My girlfriend now says I've got a terrible temper and I think it stems from that. I have mood swings and I get mad at really silly things. When my father got drunk it would annoy me and I would just lash out.

Isolation

Four young people and a few parents mentioned problems of social isolation in childhood as one effect of parental drinking. The connection was made in various ways, but was most often explained in terms of the child's wish to stay at home, whether to protect or accompany the non-drinker, monitor and supervise the drinker, or simply keep an eye on developments:

> *Father* - She was backwards in coming forwards as far as friendships with people, she just wasnae interested. And that's an effect as well, because I think she was frightened of going out wi' her friends and coming back and finding me drunk. But if she was there, you know, I wouldnae go oot for a drink. See, I'd the opportunity - 'If you go out with your friends, I can nip alang to the pub and get a few pints.' I think about it later, not at the time, I think maybe that's some of the reasons she would say 'No, I'm not going out. If I don't go oot, you've got to stay here and take care of me' sort of thing.

In addition, need for secrecy inhibited the development of friendships:

> Sometimes, I did find it difficult to have friends. I don't know if that was the alcohol and I was embarrassed and didn't know what to say. The major thing was I didn't want anybody to come into my house. I thought 'Here we go again.' I don't want anybody to come in because he's been drinking and it was an embarrassing situation.

Social isolation tends to be cumulative. Children who do not mix regularly with others may fail to develop the social skills necessary to establish later relationships.

Substance abuse

Most of the children in the sample had experimented at some point with sips or glasses of wine, as do children in the general population (Fossey, 1994). There were no apparent ill-effects, apart from one Primary child who claimed to have been drunk after drinking 'a cup of cider'.

More serious drinking was admitted by young adults. All the young men interviewed reported that they had followed the family patterns of heavy drinking, in some cases also engaging in drug misuse. Two of the young adults had established histories of substance abuse and were currently serving prison sentences for offences related to this. These young adults interpreted the link between their drinking and that of their parents in various ways but all maintained that it had had an impact. One young man said he had always sworn he would never drink, but started at the age of 18, sometimes downing 11 pints in a night. He told the interviewer 'It must be in the blood'. Another implied that it was partly a learned behaviour and that exposure to very high levels of parental consumption led him to believe that his own consumption was not problematic:

> *Interviewer* - Did you ever think 'I mustn't drink because I'll turn out like them?'. Did that thought cross your mind?
> *Young adult* - No. That never crossed my mind, because I didna think I would take it as bad as they got into it. I know I was heavily into the drink, but I wasna quite as bad as my Dad and my step-Mum.

The following quotation reveals how a young woman saw herself as deterred from drinking by her family history, yet she also acknowledged having been drunk previously, which suggests the mixed influence of parental drinking on her own experiences:

> *Interviewer* - What effect has the drinking had on you?

Young adult - Well, I cannot touch the stuff, it makes me sick. You certainly see the things it can do to a family and people round about you and it really puts you off. I mean, I have been really steamin' a few times and what I do is I'm sick down the toilet. I mean, I don't know how people could get aggressive when they drink, cause I mean, you're so paralytic.

Lost childhood

The final theme, mentioned by three young adults was the sense of having missed out on vital components of childhood. Not only can drinking episodes lead to 'child-like' parental behaviour in the short-term, but over an extended period heavy drinking can mean that a child fails to experience normal aspects of parenting and childhood such as affection, guidance and stability. This sense of loss was based on images of 'ordinary' children's experiences as happy and cherished which may overlook other causes of unhappiness or exploitation in childhood. The common image of childhood as a contented and innocent time is open to question (Ennew, 1986; Qvortrup et al., 1994). Nevertheless, the feelings of comparative deprivation in early life shaped views of their personal history and identity.

A young woman felt that she and her sister had 'grown up too quickly'. She added: 'I remember sitting saying to myself "I wish I had a Mum and Dad like everyone else" '. A young man felt he had missed out on having a parent who was 'there' for him, to give love and to confide in (his mother was a lone parent and a drinker). Another felt he had never belonged to a 'proper family' and regretted the fact that his father never spent time with him as a child:

> He used to be drunk all the time. When I was a wee boy he never ever done nothing wi' us, you know. Like when I say he never done nothing wi' us.. what I mean is - it was never like a family, you know.

His father, now long abstinent, pointed out both the long-term effects that parental drinking can have and the possibility of recovery from them:

> Barry was sort of crying and he started to say 'You never told me you loved me. All I can remember is you drinkin' - you never told me you loved me or cared for me'. ... It just shows, there's still healing going on frae the drinking days. I was never one I could say to people that I loved them. I couldnae show affection and couldnae accept it back.

A mother pointed to a change in the opposite direction, when early experiences of caring and affection were lost to her daughter's recall. This woman expressed regret that her youngest daughter could not remember the 'Good Dad' which her father had been before he succumbed to heavy drinking: 'She's never seen the real man, the really nice man that I married'.

Positive effects

The preceding section has focused on the negative long-term effects of parental heavy drinking, because the emotional hurt experienced by children was a major theme in most of the interviews. However, it is important to point out the other side of the coin. There were some individuals in the sample who seemed little affected by their parents' drinking or who even thought that in the long run it had had some positive spin-offs. A number of older Secondary children and young adults were doing well, educationally and socially. They had enjoyed school, were making good progress and had a range of friends and social interests. Either they were described by their parents as cheerful, positive people, or seemed so in interview. That is not to deny that they had been emotionally hurt in some respects and at some times by the drinking.

In addition, some were able to identify positive long-term effects of having lived through the experience. In two families where children had been high achievers at school, this was attributed to them deliberately diverting attention from the drinking. Others mentioned enhanced coping skills and greater maturity. Two of the young adults felt they had achieved greater insight into other people's problems and two Secondary girls were identified by their mother as people to whom others turned to in distress. Finally, some families clearly felt parents and children had been brought closer together by the difficult experiences they had been through.

Much larger surveys have similarly concluded that children are not necessarily doomed by heavy parental drinking to lead unsatisfactory lives or repeat their parents' life-styles (Velleman and Orford, 1993b). This is an encouraging message which it is important for children in this situation to know so they do not feel despondent about their own prospects. At the same time, there are plenty of indications that the short-term distress for many children and the long-term hurt done to some warrant outside help. The UN Convention on the Rights of the Child makes it clear that society should take action to afford children protection from harm and provide appropriate services, when parents for whatever reason are not able to meet their welfare needs. In the following chapter, we examine the kinds of formal assistance the families in the study experienced and wanted.

Summary

A number of themes emerged from older respondents' views on the long-term impact of parental drinking on personality and functioning. These were predominantly negative and included educational failure, antisocial behaviour, social isolation, heavy drinking and drug misuse, and a sense of lost childhood. However, a number of older children and young adults seemed to be leading positive, sociable lives. A few even identified beneficial side-effects arising from the experience of having a drunken parent, such as enhanced academic motivation, improved coping skills, concern for others in difficulty and greater family closeness.

8 Services - past, present and future

So far we have considered the impact on children of parental heavy drinking and its associated problems, and the personal, family and network resources which help children cope. We now consider existing services and ideas about future service provision for children of problem drinkers. This chapter is based on the experience and perspectives of the children and parents interviewed. Chapter 9 affords an additional perspective by reporting the views of professionals. The implications of the whole study for service planning and provision are discussed in the final chapter.

Current services for adults: their philosophies and consumer responses

Between them, the families in the sample had been consumers of a wide range of services geared to helping adults with drinking problems, but hardly any had obtained direct help for the children. Hence we are in a position to report extensive consumer feedback only on adult services, though some of these affected children indirectly. However we did ask about the kinds of services for children which family members thought would be helpful and we shall summarise some of their ideas about this, after we have described the services we encountered and learned about during the study.

Two points should be borne in mind. First, agencies have differing philosophies which can greatly influence the perceptions of the individuals who use them. Secondly, families who were referred to the study and were willing to talk with us are likely to have been mainly the agencies' 'successes'.

The main divide in 'treatment philosophies' for alcohol problems is between those which advocate total abstinence as the long-term solution and those who espouse a 'harm-reduction' philosophy which involves a shift to controlled 'social drinking'.

Total abstinence organisations

Two of these had been used by families in this study - the AA network and Stauros. Both view total abstinence as the only effective answer to alcohol misuse. They also shared a common approach to recovery which placed great value on membership of a close-knit supportive network providing information, advice, support and peer pressure to help achieve and sustain abnegation of alcoholic drinks.

The AA network This is a self-help organisation for 'alcoholics' centred on Alcoholics Anonymous. Whereas the other services and projects we came across were quite localised in origin and catchment area, the AA network operates on a national and indeed international level. It is run entirely by survivors, i.e. former heavy drinkers. A coherent framework has been worked out and published which delineates twelve steps on the way to complete recovery (Al-Anon Family Groups, 1986).

AA is popularly associated with the 'disease' model of 'alcoholism'. This suggests that each drinker has an individual illness from which they require to be cured. One of the key elements of treatment is membership of a close-knit group which offers support, advice and peer pressure to help sustain recovery. As Velleman (1992) points out, 'many people find AA almost evangelical, and it has both the benefits and drawbacks of that: it can turn people away, or it can lead to great commitment to that group and to the philosophy' (p. 20). However, Miller and Kurtz (1994) warn against stereotyped thinking about AA. They point out that it embraces a complex, multi-causal view of alcohol abuse. They argue that its defining characteristic is the emphasis on holistic, spiritual development within a supportive community.

AA was originally set up to help drinkers themselves. However, it has developed a network of organisations to help family members cope with the presence of a problem drinker in their midst. Al-Anon is for partners and adult offspring, Al-Ateen offers support to children and teenagers (Al-Anon Family Groups, 1986).

Unfortunately, our efforts to recruit families for the study from amongst those currently involved with either AA or Al-Anon were unsuccessful, because of these organisations' emphasis on strict anonymity. There were two drinkers we met through other channels who had belonged to AA in the past. Though they had 'moved on' from it and were no longer members, they felt it had been very helpful at the time. However, other drinkers had tried it once and been put off by its approach. It seems that it has a very useful function for those who take to it, but it is not for everyone.

Stauros was initially described to us as a 'Christian version of AA'. However, it appears to be a very different sort of organisation. It shares the belief in total abstinence, is run by survivors and has a strong and explicitly Christian spiritual basis. However, there the similarity ends. Stauros rejects the medical model of alcoholism as an illness, seeing problem drinking and drug addiction as responses to a spiritual void. They believe that bringing Christ into a person's life is the way to achieve sober and contented living. It seems to be a more open organisation than AA, though confidentiality is still important. It operates nation-wide, with many local branches, and carries out a mix of individual and group counselling. It helps partners as well as drinkers. It does no direct work with children, though representatives do outreach work, speaking to schools and youth groups about the dangers of alcohol.

We were able to recruit two families who had used Stauros, one currently, one in the past. Both spoke very warmly of it. One felt it had transformed their lives; the other that it had been a significant help.

Pros and cons of AA and Stauros The present and former members of these two organisations plus the young adult mentioned in the previous chapter illustrate the potentially helpful role of strong, coherent belief-systems in combating problem drinking. As previously mentioned, the recovery phase is frequently a difficult one for drinkers and their families; alcohol leaves a gap behind it which is hard to fill and a whole new way of life has to be constructed. A strong belief system, accompanied by regular rituals and a ready made alternative social network, clearly meets the needs of some families. To others, by contrast, the very existence of a spiritual dimension to a programme is unappealing. Furthermore, many drinkers do not want to forgo alcohol permanently, but to learn to drink it responsibly. AA and Stauros are obviously not for them.

Agencies and groups with a social drinking model

Most projects used by families in the sample hold that it is possible and sufficient to reduce alcohol intake to acceptable levels - to change from problem drinking to social drinking. They included SWD Addiction Units, Council on Alcohol programmes, Detoxification Units and NHS Addiction Clinics. In these projects excessive alcoholic drinking is looked on not as a disease or a spiritual lack, but as a behaviour that has been learned and can therefore be unlearned (Heather and Robertson, 1986). However, most workers also consider total abstinence to be a useful option for some drinkers either as a stepping stone to moderate social drinking or as a permanent solution. Permanent abstinence is strongly advocated by some social work and health professionals (Smith 1989).

Current services for children: philosophies and user views

During the course of the study we learned of three projects which are geared exclusively to children's needs, as well as three others which include direct work with children as one of their secondary functions. Two of each are located in the Glasgow area. Although our information about services was largely confined to the West of Scotland, our indirect contacts suggested that the pattern of few and isolated developments is quite typical (see also Velleman, 1993a). As far as we could tell, the six initiatives have been developed largely independently of one another. This seems to reflect the absence of any co-ordinated policy by government, voluntary agencies or self-help groups directed at children of drinking parents, with the partial exception of the AA network. Unfortunately, none of these schemes were able to introduce us to families with children who were currently using the service. Our views of them are therefore largely based on interviews with project staff. Like most new initiatives, these services were in a state of evolution. Therefore changes are to be expected in some of the details given in the following section, which apply to the time of the fieldwork in the spring of 1995.

Direct services for children and young people

Al-Ateen As mentioned above, this is a national organisation and part of the AA network. It is geared to helping children of alcoholics, primarily from mid-teens onwards. It follows the AA model. Groups are run by 'survivors', with strict anonymity and closed networking. The groups are structured but open-ended as regards length of membership. In order to ease guilt, members are taught that their parents' drinking is not their responsibility and that there is nothing they can do about it. Instead they are helped to find ways of managing the situation so that they can survive in it, with an emphasis on detachment, insight and the development of coping skills. The two young adults we interviewed who had belonged to Al-Ateen spoke in very positive terms of the organisation. In addition to helping them cope with parental drinking, one young woman had acquired important social support, whilst another reported having improved in confidence and coping skills.

SCAD (Support for Children of Adult Drinkers) This organisation came to our attention through a newspaper article and is based in the rural area of Hereford and Worcester. No consumer views were available, but the project co-ordinator was interviewed by phone. It was originally intended to be a peer-led direct support service to children, but problems with volunteers and a low rate of self-referrals led to a rethink. The remit was modified to providing support to young drinkers, promoting alcohol awareness in schools, collaborating with other agencies which support young people and counselling anyone referred as a result of these other activities. SCAD also run a limited telephone help line. The project consists of a team of volunteers led by a full-time counsellor with secretarial support. As at Al-Ateen, young people are informed at the outset that SCAD cannot change their parents' drinking. Children are encouraged not to feel guilty but get on with their own lives.

ASK (Alcohol Support Services for Kids, formerly the Children's Addiction Support Project) This too is a local organisation serving a small area of Glasgow which has high levels of deprivation and alcohol abuse. The name is ambiguous, but in fact ASK offers support to children whose parents have alcohol problems, not to children who are drinking or using drugs themselves. Established and run by Strathclyde Social Work Department, it obtains the majority of its referrals from social workers. Many come as a result of involvement with the Scottish Children's Hearings system. ASK is staffed by a project leader, three part-time counsellors and a homemaker. It deals with 30-40 school age children at any one time and is open from 8.45-4.45 on weekdays. Children are offered a two-stage service:

> 1) Activity groups of ten weeks which are not focused on alcohol and allow children the 'child time' which many have missed, as well as winning their trust. There are trips and outings as well as arts and crafts.

> 2) Closed groups of four to five children, grouped by age. These are much more structured and do focus on alcohol, as well as other problems. The aims are to allow children to 'come out' about parental drinking, identify sources of informal support and learn coping strategies.

A few children in addition receive individual counselling. The Homemaker gives practical support to the family and offers the children a befriending service which includes trips and treats.

Unfortunately, we were unable to recruit any family from this project to our sample. We did, however, meet a group of four young people aged 14-16 who were currently attending the project. They were very positive about the service, particularly the activities, which work well as an initial attraction. The children said it was helpful to realise that other children were facing similar problems to their own. One-to-one sessions with counsellors were also regarded as very useful, enabling them to talk over worries in a confidential setting. According to staff the young people do not support each other much with respect to problems at home, but enjoy each other's company. Thus the group experience seems to be as much compensatory as therapeutic. Again, these teenagers had learnt a philosophy akin to that of AA and SCAD, namely that children cannot stop parents drinking and that it is not their fault. This helps to dispel self-blame.

Services which have secondary contacts with children

A number of organisations whose primary function is helping adults with drinking problems also have some contact with children. We met representatives from three of them.

GEAAP (Greater Easterhouse Alcohol and Addiction Project) This is a service run by the Glasgow Council on Alcohol, and its main remit is counselling for adults in an area with high levels of alcohol abuse. However, two workers organise an outreach/educational programme whose purpose is to discourage youngsters from developing heavy drinking habits. Access to accurate information and positive role models are seen as key requirements. The programme is aimed at children of ten and over in local Primary and Secondary schools. Using a health education model, the workers attempt to increase children's awareness of alcohol and its effects by means of presentations, exercises and group discussions. The children are not actively encouraged to discuss parental drinking or to come forward for help with this. Anyone who asks is told to phone GEAAP if they want to, but very few have done so.

Besides this school based programme, counsellors from GEAAP's adult alcohol counselling service also occasionally give support directly to a few children whose parents are receiving help. We interviewed one family from this project. Both the drinker and the non-drinking partner said they had received high quality support, but there had been no contact with their son. The counsellor had hoped to introduce us to a family where the 13-year-old girl had also received individual counselling, but she refused to meet us as did two other children whose parents had given permission for them to be seen.

The Aberlour Child Care Trust This Scottish voluntary organisation provides a range of support services for families. These include a residential facility in Glasgow to help mothers with addiction problems. Most of their work is with mothers misusing drugs, but the centre also deals with cases of alcohol abuse. A maximum of six families can stay at any one time. They live in residential flats for 6-12 months and there they receive intensive support. The children go into these residential recovery units with their mothers and attend local schools. They also take part in individual counselling, group activities and various outings. When parents have been discharged from the Project, the children can continue to drop in at the centre. It is open 24 hours a day and staff are on call at all hours.

We were unable to meet any children from this project, but one mother we interviewed felt her children had gained from it. Features which had been especially helpful to them included the relaxed, caring atmosphere; the policy of being 'open all hours'; the sanctuary it afforded to children who could go there at any time independently to escape parental violence.

Family and Alcohol Project, Edinburgh This time-limited project is fully funded by The Scottish Office as part of their Minimal Intervention Programme, but located in Lothian Social Work Department offices. It is staffed by one project leader, who is a trained social worker, and one nurse. Referrals are from social work teams and family centres. The aim is to offer brief intervention to families where there is a drink issue. Older children are included in family discussions if they and their parents are willing. However major issues are not raised with them as this is seen as more appropriately done by the professional who has long-term contact. It appears that the early response rate from referring agencies has not been good.

This agency was unable to give us access to families, as they were already being seen as part of another ongoing evaluation. Hence, we have no consumer perspective.

Services planned

Although these were the only services for children we encountered, we learned of other agencies, both statutory and voluntary, who were planning to introduce them. Several stated a wish that this aspect of their work should be strengthened. It seemed that services to children was an area of service development very much in the minds of alcohol agencies.

Services desired

The final parts of our interviews with children, parents, young adults and professionals dealt with their views on what might be the best ways to meet the needs of children living with parents who have alcohol-related problems. Parents and children based their ideas for services mainly on what would or could have been most useful to them personally, though some young adults took a broader perspective. The needs identified were very diverse, with children facing different problems and being at different stages of readiness to respond to any outside intervention. The main suggestions from children, young adults and parents are outlined below. The views of professionals are given separately in Chapter 9, and incorporated in the concluding chapter of the book. Their ideas were often quite similar to those of families.

Specific services proposed

Drop-in Centre (Suggested by one child, two young adults, three parents) This would be an informal centre, open to anyone, 'something like a social club'. The aim would be to deal with particular problems by offering a general-purpose, non-stigmatising service, accessible and attractive to local residents and building on people's strengths, as in the community development type of family centres described by Holman (1988). Activity based, it would have a play area for younger children and other activities for older children (arts, crafts, pool table, football and other active sports). The centre would provide somewhere to go to get out of the house and an opportunity to mix with others. In this way, trust could be built up in other children and in workers, as a prelude to individual confiding if that was desired. One parent pointed out the dearth of activities to escape to in rural areas, especially at the critical times of Sunday and Saturday nights. A teenage boy stressed the value of strenuous activities to work off pent-up feelings. The need for younger children to have somewhere to go was also pointed out. Particularly in urban areas, there are usually already youth clubs and other places that adolescents can escape to, but nothing for younger ones. In rural areas, the converse may be true.

Individual counselling (Suggested by two children, two young adults and three parents) It was suggested that many children would benefit from talking about their problems and expressing their feelings to a sympathetic adult. Since family members are often closely involved with the problem, it is often easier to do this with someone outside the family. This outsider was usually seen as either a trained worker or someone who had been through a similar experience, but come to terms with their own feelings about it. A combination of the two was seen as ideal.

Children will be at different stages of readiness to confide; some will immediately take the opportunity to 'let it all pour out'; others will need a period of non-threatening 'fun' and activity before they can do so. Two Secondary age sisters said:

> *Child 1* - Some children would (need this) because they haven't taken it too well. But others might have taken it not too badly. They might not need that.
> *Child 2* - I think it would be a good idea. I don't suppose you'd ever forget what happened, but it would help you cope with it a bit better.

Some parents hoped that individual sessions with the child would be accompanied or followed by advice to them as to how best to deal with the child's fears, anger and anxiety.

Family mediation (Suggested by two parents, but interestingly no children or young adults) These parents agreed that individual counselling would be helpful to children, but hoped it might also lead on, if appropriate, to establishing or restoring communication between parents and child. One said:

> I think it would be good for Laura to talk to a counsellor, somebody who understands these situations, and explain to that person how she feels, what she feels, what kind of questions she'd like to ask and how to go about speaking to her parents. If she's got anger against me or her mother. And then maybe everybody sits doon wi' the counsellor and Laura gets a free go and she can say whatever she likes. ... The counsellor as a go-between, you know? See, I would like to sit down with Laura and clear the air, but it's difficult to start. You don't know where to start. ... It would also help the parents. You're really hearing for the first time how they feel. Because we love our kids and we'll dae anything for them, but we tend to forget that they've got minds, they've got worries, and they've got problems.

Groupwork (Suggested by three children, one young adult and four parents) A few children mentioned this spontaneously, but more agreed with the idea when prompted. However, two children said they would never attend a group like this themselves. Those in favour believed that meeting other children in the same situation could reduce feelings of being 'the only one' and provide support. In all just over half the children in the sample voiced the wish to meet others in the same position:

> I would have liked to have met with other people, so I would have known that my Mum was not the only one.

This was a need also recognised retrospectively by some young adults.
  Parents who favoured groups had often themselves experienced the benefit of one. They noted that groups can be fun, as well as a rewarding experience. There is the chance to contribute and help others. Peer support was thought to help reticent children to open up:

> *Father* - Somewhere they can go and play for part of the day, but they can also go into a group session and just speak freely, because - it takes a lot to get things out of children and I find if you put them into a room with just one person it's difficult. He hauds a lot to hisself and I think he would haud too much, he wouldnae let it all

oot. Whereas if he was with other kids, it would enable him to speak as well. He would open up, I feel he would open up.

As with individual counselling, it was considered that group workers should have been through the experience themselves, be specially trained or both.

A help line (Suggested by one young adult and two parents) It was recognised that children could feel inhibited about approaching an agency and identifying themselves as having such a sensitive and stigmatising problem in their family. Parental disapproval or fear of repercussions, peer pressure and sense of shame could all deter children from going to a project door. Particularly in rural areas, small integrated communities can make the process of seeking help highly visible, whilst distance, cost and transport difficulties make it impossible for children to get to urban centres independently. A freephone line was seen as one way around this; available to any child with access to a phone box, confidential, anonymous and free. It would be important to have the phone staffed on a 24 hour basis by trained personnel or survivors, since crises tend to arise mainly at night or weekends. Counselling could be given over the phone, as an end in itself, or as a prelude to seeking face-to-face help from other sources. The idea is familiar to children through ChildLine. It could be more realistic to widen the scope of an existing help line than to find resources for one dedicated to drink-related issues only.

Education initiatives (Suggested by three parents) It is perhaps not a coincidence that this approach was recommended only by adults. A few parents felt that in addition to help for individual children, there was a need for education for children in general about the effects of alcohol and the need to manage it responsibly. This was seen as necessary to counteract the commercial and media pressures to consume. One mother, from a heavy drinking culture went further and felt children also needed education in the value of what she saw as normal family life, but which her children had no experience of:

> What would be ideal - I don't know if this is anything to do with how their project is gonna be - is to let kids know how a family should be. To let him know that a family means a Mum and Dad both doing things at home, equally and no' this carry on wi' Mum does all the housework, makes all the dinners, goes all the shops, pays all the bills, which is all they've ever saw. And Dad just goes to his work and comes back wi' a drink in him. I would like them to be aware that there's more to family life than just that. Because I can't really say that there's any other sort of even examples that they know of that's any different to our family. Everyone I know is separated or

the man drinks. There's no one that's a happy family, really. And I would like young children, growing up, to know what a family's all about. What Mum should be doing, what Dad could be doing - all that. What my two know is people are either one parent families or the Dad always drinks. To get a bit of education about what family life could be.

Issues and dilemmas concerning service provision

In addition to the suggestions about specific types of service outlined above, a number of more general points were raised about the nature of service provision for children of problem drinkers.

Help from adult 'survivors' of parental alcoholism There was strong support from both parents and children for the idea that staff working on these initiatives should have 'been there' themselves; preferably young adults who had themselves had a drinking parent. This was thought to add credibility in the eyes of youngsters and to help real understanding of the problems faced:

> I think it would also help if they'd had the experience themselves - like somebody in their family so they would know what you were going through.

However, it was stressed that experience is not everything. Survivors also need to be properly trained (or work alongside a professional) and they need to have 'worked through' their own experience before trying to help other children with theirs. It was also pointed out by a survivor parent that the testimony of survivors is only helpful if it stresses the positive (recovery) aspect of experience, rather than harping on the negative.

Location of services The location of a project was considered important, but it appeared to be hard to please everyone. Some thought it should be in a neighbourhood shopping precinct for easy local access, others in a central city location near a bus route, so that a wider population could be served. One drawback of a centralised service could be that children would not be allowed to travel to it independently. On the other hand, a specialised neighbourhood service, though is easy to get to, lacks anonymity for those who would wish to keep their attendance secret. There appears to be no easy answer to this.

Independent versus bolt-on services Two parents argued that it would be best for a project to be linked to an existing service, particularly a counselling service for adults with drinking problems. Referrals could be readily made from families already in touch and it would be easy to carry out 'parallel work' with parents and child. That would ensure that the parental drinking was treated, as well as the child's anxieties. On the other hand, many children need help whose parents do not admit to a drinking problem and these would be excluded. They might be more readily recruited to a separate service.

Names/identity   The question of what a specialist centre should be called was considered crucial, but again we came up with dilemmas rather than a consensus. In one view it should be vague and above all have no mention of parental drinking, to avoid stigmatising those who attended or deterring children who would feel ashamed if 'labelled' in this way:

> *Mother (ID)* - Likes of myself, right, if I go to see (counsellor) up at (office), it's a big building and that kind of thing is a stigma attached to it kind of. So if it was something not kind of like that, somewhere the kids could go to that wasn't ... Because I don't care who it is, or what child - it is, they - if they think they're going somewhere and they're going into this building and everybody knows 'Her Mum and Dad must have a drink problem' that kind of way. I don't know how you get round that kind of thing, cause if you've got a place where children can go to speak to somebody - as soon as someone sees them going in there, they'll say 'Oof! They know exactly, you know.

In contrast, there was seen to be a danger in failing to be honest about the true nature of the project. An agency which plays down its ultimate aims in order to be unthreatening may hamper workers' ability to raise the issue of drinking with parents, when this seems to be appropriate.

A specialist or more general service?   In view of some of the difficulties associated with a specialist service targeted at children of problem drinkers, an alternative suggestion was to provide help within the context of a broader family or youth service. It was pointed out that parents who drink often have other problems too, which the child may need help in coping with (such as separation or psychiatric illness). Not only might this reach a wider or different group of children, but the coping skills and insights gained could be applied to many situations, not just parental drinking. On the other hand, the presence of children with other less stigmatised parental problems might inhibit those with drinking parents from 'coming out' about this.

Connections with statutory agencies   A few parents considered that a strong impediment to use of a project would be parental fears that children would reveal family secrets which might result in them being taken away for their own protection. In particular, any Social Work Department involvement in the Project was thought by some to be a deterrent, because of its association in their minds with compulsory removal of children from home:

> *Father* - And a lot of people don't like authority as well, because they're scared. I used to be that way as well and I think if you'd have came to me a few year ago and asked me the same thing, I would have said no, Colin wasnae going, because at the time, I'd have been feart that social services would get involved and maybe taking Colin away - that kind of thing worries people. I think if they got that through, that there wouldnae be that kinda thing, that as you say when you came last week, the only time that you would inform them was if the child was in danger. If that was put through to people, I think they would know their children wasnae going to get taken off the. I think you'd need to stress that, because that's a big, big fear.

In practice links with a Social Work or Social Services Department may work both ways. Some parents may be reluctant to allow their children to attend because of the connection. On the other hand, a project such as ASK receives many referrals through social workers because of its position. Even independent projects have to face the issue of potential revelations of abuse, as we did as researchers, so that careful thought and clarification would be required concerning confidentiality and anonymity.

Need for pro-active recruitment Even if parents did not prevent a child from attending a project, there could be resistance from children themselves. One teenage girl felt she could not have approached a project directly, but would have welcomed involvement if an already trusted worker had taken the initiative in suggesting she should go:

> *Child* - I wouldn't have liked to approach them, I don't think. If somebody was seeing somebody about drinking, like my Dad was seeing Cathy (a Community Psychiatric Nurse) ... I might have wanted Cathy to get me to see somebody but I wouldn't' have liked to step forward myself and say 'Gonnae ask somebody to ask ma Dad to ask Cathy if there's anybody.'
> *Interviewer* - You'd have liked Cathy to come to you and say 'Would you like to talk to somebody?'
> *Child* - Yes.

A mother in a different family said she would not have encouraged attendance at a project, but would have been happy for her children to go if they had been persuaded it was a good idea and asked her permission. Some young adults recalled that when younger they would have been reluctant to get involved with a helping agency because they felt ashamed or shared their family's hostility to 'the authorities'.

Identification of cases Attracting children into a project was considered to be a problem, because families sought to hide their difficulties from outsiders. Referrals could come from child and family support or alcohol treatment agencies, but that would only apply to children in touch with them. It was stressed that a suitable project also needs to reach out to children whose parents are receiving no help at all. Waiting for self-referrals to come in could be a slow process. One suggestion from two young adults was that teachers could act as a link. Children often confide in them, particularly in primary school. Another proposal from two parents and one young adult was to leaflet schools in a routine manner, perhaps as part of an alcohol awareness programme. If every child in the school received a leaflet about the project with reassurance about confidentiality and a freephone number, this could avoid any feeling of being 'singled out'. It would be easy to explain at home - 'Oh, everybody got one'.

> I think a good way would be at school level. There wasn't anybody came to my school and said 'If there's anybody with a problem...?'. I mean I'm quite sure I probably wouldn't have went. I don't know, maybe I might have went but if there was someone there saying 'We're from the national group who's there to help anybody whose got a problem with an alcoholic parent. It will be very confidential. If you want to speak to us, we'll give everybody a leaflet and all you have to do is take it home, write out your name and address and send it to us.' Everybody would be getting a leaflet so nobody would be singled out. A national thing going to youth clubs, going to schools, all these things and saying 'Everybody is getting a leaflet' rather than say 'If you've got a problem, pick up a leaflet as you go out', because then you would be recognised.

Nature of the help needed Finally, three people specified the ideas they would most wish to get across to children, whatever the structure of the service. One young woman (from Al-Ateen) felt the most important thing was to help children realise they can't stop the parent drinking and are not responsible for it. However, two partners of drinkers felt that children primarily needed help to understand why the drinking parent acted as he/she did. This was seen as important to help children distinguish between the 'real' parent and the effects of drink; in other words, to hate the sin and not the sinner. It could also help children to understand that negative behaviour apparently directed at them is prompted by other things. For example, one partner thought many children must feel they are not loved and need to be helped to understand that drinkers may despise themselves and that this is why they cannot show love to others.

Summary

A variety of services are readily available for adult drinkers, many of which were used by parents in the sample. They are based on differing ideologies concerning the nature and causes of problem drinking and hence appropriate ways of helping. Alcohol misuse can be seen as an illness, a response to a spiritual void or a learned behaviour.

By contrast, there are only a few existing services for children of problem drinkers. They usually have small catchment areas, so that children in most areas have no local facilities available. The projects vary greatly in structure and intervention methods, but tend to share an ideology that children cannot and should not influence parental drinking since they are not to blame and so not responsible. They aim to provide compensatory activities, advice and support.

Very few children or young adults in the sample had received any form of formal support with parental drinking. Nearly all those interviewed thought some kind of service was desirable, but their needs and specific proposals were quite diverse, which indicates a requirement for a flexible and tiered service. Their suggestions included drop-in centres, individual counselling, group work, a freephone help line and educational initiatives. They raised a number of pertinent issues relating to staffing, location, identity and content of a service. Several obstacles to identification and recruitment were noted. Since our sample families was probably more open to help than most, this is a vital consideration which reinforces the need for multiple means and stages for making assistance available.

9 Professional perspectives

Introduction

Although the primary focus of the study was on the views of children and parents, we recognised the value of practitioners' perspectives. Therefore a small number of interviews were carried out with key workers in the field, for two main reasons. Firstly they gave an additional perspective on the topic. Secondly they provided indirect information on a wider range of families than we were able to reach in our own sample. To tap into this pool of experience we carried out a series of systematic interviews with 15 professionals from 8 different agencies. The same broad themes were discussed as in the family interviews. Several of the professionals had a specific remit to support children in coping with parental drinking, others sometimes worked with such children as part of a wider remit. The agencies involved were:

- 3 agencies directly supporting children of drinking parents

- 2 agencies supporting families with drinking problems

- 1 agency supporting women with drink and drug problems

- 1 agency offering refuge to women and children

- 1 school-based agency supporting children with a variety of problems

The views of the professionals interviewed supported many of the findings from the family interviews. However, as anticipated, there were some divergences and additions. In summarising their perspectives, we shall use the same headings as previous chapters in order to highlight similarities and differences compared with the families' perceptions.

Problem drinking patterns

Professionals observed that class and gender differences exist in patterns of heavy drinking and responses to it. One worker suggested that middle class norms, which value verbal coherence and controlled behaviour, lead to a greater degree of shame and concealment of heavy drinking. Hence, in middle class families parental drinking is more likely to be a hidden problem.

In the main the professionals we met spoke about drinking in areas of social and economic deprivation where their projects were located. Several said that in their experience heavy drinking was a cultural norm for working class men, particularly those living in areas of poverty. In this context, the ability to 'take a drink' was regarded as an indicator of masculinity. They pointed to a tradition of men getting drunk outside the home after work on Friday or Saturday night as a socially encouraged activity. With rising unemployment, mid-week daytime drinking has also become culturally acceptable. Men drink to fill in time, particularly on Tuesdays or Wednesdays after the receipt of their weekly benefit.

In contrast with this view of excessive drinking by individuals as an extension of common norms, female heavy drinking by women was seen to represent a deviation from expectations. Daytime drinking by mothers was said to be particularly frowned on, since it contradicts ideals of them as homemakers and carers. The taboo which surrounds female heavy drinking was said to lead to greater secrecy and denial. One worker had found that children are usually more open about fathers' drinking than about mothers'. Professionals considered that women, particularly mothers, tended to drink in response to stresses, both psychological and situational (poor housing, child care responsibilities, poverty). One worker considered that drinking mothers often suffered from low self esteem, unable to assert themselves or to make their needs known except when drunk.

Several agreed that among families living in poverty heavy drinking, whether by mothers or fathers, was often just one item in a package of problems which they displayed, including poor relationships, violence and disorganised lifestyles.

Direct impact on the child

Professionals claimed that, in the deprived areas they worked in, many children regard heavy drinking as entirely normal, particularly by fathers. In the short term this can lessen the impact on the child or even result in its being seen as positive. Fathers may return from the pub on Fridays and Saturdays sleepy and with slurred speech, but in a genial, relaxed mood, bearing sweets, toys and other small treats. Heavy drinking can thus be seen as 'fun'. Where paternal heavy drinking is the norm, children are less likely to experience a sense of stigma or social isolation as a result. On the other hand, children with drinking mothers were reported to face teasing at school, exacerbated by the fact that in poor housing schemes there is little privacy, so that family problems readily become common knowledge. Our family interviews showed there is some truth in these stereotypcial representations, but significant exceptions occur, too.

Some professionals commented that through exposure to parental and neighbourhood drinking, many children from an early age have a sophisticated awareness of alcohol and its effects. They considered that other workers can underestimate children's knowledge and understanding. Consequently, they are overprotective of the children, failing to raise the subject with them and excluding them from discussions on the problem. This benignly intended avoidance denies children the support they need in coping with a situation in which they are already heavily involved and probably playing an active role. One worker suggested that many children do not at the time see themselves as passive victims of parental drinking, though they may retrospectively re-evaluate their experiences in such terms later in life. These comments seem to argue for more efforts to give even young children the opportunity to participate in any support and treatment programmes offered to their parents.

Professionals agreed with many of the negative direct effects of parental drinking on children reported in the literature and observed in our sample. They spoke of children witnessing violence to partners and to the home. Many experience fear and anxiety, particularly from the unpredictability of drunken behaviour. For example, will the parent simply fall asleep or launch into a fight? Some children were said to be chronically nervous, tense, wary and watchful, constantly trying to "size up" the family situation. Anxiety and embarrassment over what might happen inhibits children from bringing friends home. They have a feeling that the 'home is not a home' - it is a source of danger rather than a place of refuge. Some children suffer acute anxiety over the physical effects of alcohol on the parent's health, and the very real possibility of death.

All the effects noted above were also found in our sample. However, professionals strongly emphasised other negative effects which did not emerge as major themes among our children, though some were referred to by the young adults. Among these were physical violence directed at the child, acute financial problems, children inadequately clothed or fed, hopelessness and a sense of family paralysis. Children were said to resent not having new clothes and shoes, and to be angry that there was never any money for them. Some parents were said to demonstrate a complete lack of interest in their children's education;

failing to turn up for school events, not reading school reports, not ensuring that children attended regularly.

Interestingly, verbal abuse, which seemed particularly salient to children in our sample, did not emerge as a major theme from the professional interviews. Such problems are less visible than the ones they spoke of and may also have been overshadowed by more dramatic difficulties in some cases.

These differences in emphasis served to confirm our suspicion that our sample (apart from the young adults) was largely recruited from parents who were, despite having serious drinking problems, relatively competent in the management of day to day affairs. It is equally possible, though, that professionals tend to encounter and recollect the most extreme cases. Hence each perspective is necessary to form a more rounded picture of the range of implications of excessive alcohol consumption.

Impact on family dynamics with indirect consequences for the child

The role reversal detailed in the literature and noted in our sample was also mentioned by professionals. However, their stress was on the practical responsibilities which children of drinking parents assume within the family. Children were described as regularly putting parents to bed, taking responsibility for getting younger siblings off to school, cooking, cleaning, shopping, seeing that fires and cigarettes were extinguished before going to bed. As already described, few of the children in our sample faced such tasks, probably because of the comparative competence of the drinking parent or the presence of a non-drinking partner.

However, other themes mentioned by professionals did coincide with those raised in our sample. Several described how parents' secrecy or denial about the drinking can be frustrating for children who want to talk about it. The wish to be fair to both parents can lead to stress and torn loyalties in children. Premature responsibility can lead to a sense of lost childhood.

Several professionals also stressed the problematic impact of the recovery period on family dynamics and functioning. The drinker's fight to remain sober can become self-absorbing and extremely time-consuming, so children can become marginalised. A child may also have difficulty in adjusting to the parent's sober behaviour, with stricter discipline or resumption of adult roles which the children had become accustomed to taking on. Paradoxically, children can resent their newly competent parent, since their own freedom and status may be reduced. They may need help in coping with their mixed up feelings when the apparently desirable outcome of parental sobriety leaves them feeling puzzled, frustrated or disappointed.

Coping, support and communication

Professionals' discussion of how children cope with the effects of parental drinking centred mainly on individual coping strategies, many of which were also found in our sample. In their experience, children often attempt to remove themselves from the drinking situation. Examples given included escaping from the house to a "den" or to other relatives and retreating to a bedroom or some other drinker-free zone. However, other children withdraw psychologically, 'curling in on themselves' and avoiding eye contact (which can look shifty and alienate adults). They may purposely isolate themselves from their peers to avoid teasing and stigmatising. One child was described as retreating into a fantasy world where she had much more control.

Acting out was also mentioned as a coping response, which can be positive or negative. On the positive side, some children fling themselves into outside activities, both to avoid the drinker and to release frustration. Others seek out sources of interest and success at school or in the neighbourhood. However, on the negative side, professionals cited cases of children transferring their anger onto other targets, notably school or teachers, with the result that they end up in trouble themselves. In these cases the real source of the anger was sometimes unrecognised both by the child and by those trying to help him/her, so the child's difficulties could be compounded without the main cause being tackled.

Many children were said to use denial as a coping mechanism - refusing to admit to any negative feelings about their parents' drinking. This contrasts sharply with the children in our sample who were very open with us. Admittedly a minority of our sample asserted quite definitely that the drinking did not impinge greatly on their lives and this could be interpreted as denial. However if we accord veracity to the child's own perspective, it seems more likely that some children are relatively unscathed and professionals find this hard to believe.

A few workers felt that there may be a gender difference in coping styles. Two professionals working in a school based agency, where the focus was on a range of children's difficulties, said they were less aware of girls with drinking parents. They suggested this might be because girls act out less, so their problems do not come to public attention in the way that, for example, boys' offending does. However, they also considered that parental drinking could be the unrecognised cause behind some girls' poor school attendance.

It was suggested by one professional that children cope better with parental drinking if they have the support of someone consistent and dependable, and that most children have at least one confidant. Several professionals regarded grandmothers as particularly valuable sources of support, as we also found. Some believed that siblings support each other, others that they did not help much. In contrast to the importance of peer support revealed in our family interviews, friends were not mentioned by professionals as potential sources of comfort and help. One worker stated that children would be unable to confide in peers for fear of stigmatising or teasing. It appears that teachers can become regular confidants. However, one worker felt that older children are 'wide' and 'astute', careful not to reveal family secrets to authority figures.

The impression professionals had was that communication within drinking families was usually poor. Parents tended to deny their drinking had any effect on the children, and children were loath to appear disloyal. Additionally, one worker suggested that in some families drinking is so much part of life that it does not merit comment.

Longer term implications of parental problem drinking

Professionals focused almost entirely on the negative effects of problem drinking on children's development. Several stressed its damaging effects on education. They depicted situations where children are preoccupied with family crises and cannot focus on learning, gradually falling further and further behind. Lack of family routine means that children come to school irregularly or late, ill equipped, with homework not done. This leads to negative interactions between school and family. It was also pointed out that poor school attendance can inhibit peer group acceptance; children are simply not at school enough of the time to forge good relationships, and this compounds isolation. A key implication is that more focused attention needs to be given by schools, education authorities and other agencies to the impact of parental drinking on school attendance and performance.

Some professionals considered that many children of problem drinkers were left with deep anger, hatred and resentment, which they are unable to express directly. This can lead to severe behaviour problems, which are not helped by inconsistent home discipline, with parents being strict when sober and lax when drunk. Low self esteem and self-blame were also considered problems for some children, possibly leading to attention-seeking behaviour.

Finally, two workers mentioned the poor role model that problem drinkers provide. Children who observe their parents acting selfishly, concealing and denying their actions, and resorting to alcohol as a coping strategy, learn the message that this is the adult way of life and are more likely to follow the same path themselves.

Services: past, present and future

In general, professionals asserted that services for children of problem drinkers were badly needed, though there was some disagreement as to whether this would be best provided as a separate service targeted at this specific group, or within general support services aimed at a wider population. Some also pointed out difficulties such a service might encounter.

Fears of authority, notably the fear that children may be removed, are widespread, so it was considered that a service would have most chance of success if it was clearly differentiated from any association with the Social Work or Social Services umbrella - by its name, location and philosophy. Placing a facility within a general advice centre was suggested as one way to achieve anonymity for users. It was recognised that many children might be reluctant to use the service and that parents might be equally reluctant to allow them to attend. Referrals by trusted workers could overcome this in some cases, but for 'hard to reach' families, collaboration or consultation with a key worker might be more productive than offering a direct service. Even when children come to the service it may take time to build up trust to the point that they can admit to parental drinking or to negative feelings about it, since denial and fear of the consequences of disclosure are common. Younger children may need psychological 'permission' from their parents before they feel able to talk freely to workers. Joint family sessions may also help. Even so, loyalty and denial may make it hard for children to make the link between parental drinking and negative feelings displaced elsewhere.

Whilst recognising a general need for assistance to children, several of the professionals identified particular priority groups:

- Younger children whose needs may be underestimated because they are less able to act out to make them known

- Teenage girls who need single-sex groups imparting coping skills; mixed gender groups were not thought to work well in adolescence

- Children of parents who are undergoing or have undergone Detox or rehabilitation programmes

Suggestions for particular services to help children included

- Attractive teenage counselling services which are up front about alcohol, to enable children to 'come out' about parental drinking

- One-to-one befriending services

- Drop-in centres to attract a range of children, plus structured groups for those who need/desire a specific service

- Support out of office hours to deal with crises

- Preventive work in schools and youth groups (which would have the twin benefits of educating about alcohol and providing a source of referrals)

In general, it was recognised that any service geared to the needs of this group of children will have to be flexible and varied, with the ability to respond promptly and sensitively to family crises.

Summary

Our interviews with professionals suggested that most of the themes which arose in our interviews were thought to be valid for other children of problem drinkers. However, they also suggested that many children would be less forthcoming, more reticent, and much more resistant to intervention than ours were. The interviews also confirmed that our sample may have underrepresented the practical difficulties, physical abuse and destruction of life-chances that heavy drinking brings to children. Services for children of problem drinkers will need to attend to these problems as well as to those identified in our study. Equally, professionals may be overly pessimistic about the long term effects of parental drinking on some children and may underestimate the coping skills present in many heavy drinking families.

There was much overlap in the suggestions made by children, young adults, parents and professionals about services. The implications for support to children and families will be developed in the final chapter.

10 Summary and implications - reducing the hurt

The aims and nature of the study

In the opening chapter we saw that the consumption of alcoholic drinks is very common amongst parents, with many drinking well beyond recommended limits. Whilst moderate drinking is socially approved, stigma and embarrassment is attached to drunkenness, especially if it is persistent.

There is much evidence of the harmful effects that parental alcohol misuse can have on children, though a significant proportion appear to reach adulthood relatively unscathed. However, most assessments of the impact on children have relied on statistical associations of quantified measures or on second-hand clinical accounts. A need was identified to hear directly from children themselves as well as from their parents.

Therefore a study was commissioned by the Health Education Board for Scotland and Barnardos Scotland. The study set out to explore by means of qualitative interviews with children, parents and young adults the meaning and impact for a child of living within a family where alcohol abuse is a problem. Combined with other pointers from the literature, the experiences and views revealed by the research were to form the basis for assessing the associated needs of children, the formal and informal resources and services available to them, and indications of what service and educational developments seem to be required.

It was originally planned to interview approximately 20 children and their parents about their current circumstances, plus a small number of young adults for retrospective accounts of growing up in a family with a heavy drinking parent. After a lengthy period of extensive networking and negotiation in order to recruit an adequate sample, semi-structured qualitative interviews were carried out with 27 individuals ranging in age from 5 to 28 and separate interviews with one or both parents in most instances, including all of the younger children. Eight of the children in the sample were of primary school age. At a later stage of the study, 15 professionals and a groups of four teenagers attending a specialist project also contributed their views.

The interviews were semi-structured, exploring a set of themes using open-ended questions and allowing participants to initiate and follow up themes in their own words. Some visual and verbal prompts were used with the children to help make the interviews more informal, interesting and concrete. Care was taken not to press children to discuss issues they did not wish to. Both parents and children were asked to describe the drinking, the child's responses and coping mechanisms, the availability of support and confidants, and the impact of the drinking on the child. Older teenagers and young adults were also asked to reflect with the benefit of hindsight on the long-term implications for them of their parents' drinking. These older individuals and all the parents in the study were invited to comment on family and neighbourhood patterns of drinking.

The sample of families was hard-won, because of the delicacy of the topic. Hence it was largely opportunistic and it cannot be seen as representative. Since recruitment was largely via specialist and problem-oriented agencies, and excluded children in care, the sample was skewed towards the serious end of heavy drinking, but excluded the most extreme cases where drink had contributed to longer-term substitute care.

However, the sample did cover a fair mix of household types, social backgrounds, economic circumstances and parental life-stages. Households were included in which the problem drinker was the father only, mother only and both parents, although in a few instances opinions differed as to whether a particular individual's drinking was problematic or not. Even within the relatively small sample of 20 households, there was a wide range of drink patterns as regards location, timing and frequency.

The difficulties we encountered as researchers in making contact with children of parents who misuse alcohol mirror the problems likely to be faced by anyone seeking to assist this group. The secrecy and shame which surround excessive drinking mean that both parents and children are often reluctant to let outsiders know what is happening. People who know them, including professionals, may also be protective of their privacy. Furthermore, fear of allegations of neglect or ill-treatment reinforce the reluctance to open up. Only some families with alcohol problems are in touch with specialist agencies. Some may gain help from more general purpose organisations or those dealing mainly with a different presenting problems (like Women's Aid). Even then, the children are often not the primary focus of concern. Some families with high levels of drinking have little contact with health or welfare agencies.

We shall now draw out key points and implications from the findings whilst outlining a possible framework for the development of service delivery and health education for this population. The chapter has the following structure:

- Stress, coping and supports
- Children's needs and rights
- Existing resources
- Options for resource development

Stress, coping and supports

Whether any potential difficulty manifests itself as a problem depends largely on four elements which formed a framework for the study:

1. how the event or situation is understood and perceived
2. how serious or intense it is
3. the personal capacity to deal with it
4. the amount and nature of support provided by others

This model is derived from analysis of a wide range of stressors and coping responses (McCubbin et al., 1983; Antonovsky, 1987; Krahn, 1993). There is an interaction between each of these four elements which affects the nature and severity of felt stress and the impact of that on daily functioning.

Stress

The study revealed that all the children were aware of the parental drinking, although a few did not give it the salience with which it figured in professional or even parental perceptions. Children's explanations for the drinking were nearly all 'social' rather than 'medical'. They attributed causation mainly to interpersonal or material pressures. We found little evidence of children regarding themselves as responsible for the overall drinking, although a few young adults had gone through a stage of self-blame and at least a third of the children felt guilty for 'provoking' particular drunken episodes. On the other hand, many children did feel a need to take responsibility for modifying the drinking behaviour and its consequences.

In nearly all cases the drinking was heavy enough to impair or markedly affect the behaviour and functioning of the parent. Four main patterns of drinking were found in the sample:

- constantly opportunistic
- nightly
- regular once or twice weekly
- binges

The majority of children viewed the drinking and related behaviour negatively, some very much so. There were, however, a small minority who found it amusing or endearing. A few simply took it for granted as a normal part of their lives.

Many children disliked the immediate aspects of the drinking, such as the smells and unpredictability. Common responses were worry, fear, sadness and anger. Sometimes the behaviour associated with inebriation was perceived as having qualities of silliness, lack of self-control and poor self-care which contradict expectations of adulthood and parental responsibility. This could be embarrassing, irritating or disturbing.

In the majority of the cases, the parent's behaviour combined impulsiveness with adult power to produce frightening effects. This took two forms. Firstly there was physical aggression. In this sample the violence was not directed towards the children (though it had been to some young adults). Instead it threatened and damaged the two main sources of comfort and security for a child - the other parent or the home. That the study did not detect much physical abuse related to drunkenness is probably due to the nature of the sample recruitment process, as this phenomenon is well known from the child care and protection literature (Simpson et al., 1993). The campaigns against corporal punishment are one means to combat the problem (Newell, 1993; Commission on Violence, 1995).

Secondly, there was often severe verbal abuse of children themselves. We were struck in this study by the acute distress caused to children by verbal violence and it would seem this issue requires vigorous attention. Although it is harder than physical abuse to detect and trickier to define acceptable limits, verbal abuse is also contrary to children's entitlement to respect. The resulting fear, anger of loss of confidence mean that parents can harm their children without laying a finger on them. The invisible damage which can be produced by insults and ridicule is conveyed in this quote from Newson and Newson (1976) ' "Sticks and stones may break my bones, but words can never hurt me!" ' cries the child with bravado. Hurt you? They'll mark you for life.' (pp. 370-1).

Coping and supports

It seemed that many parents had genuine concern for their children. Several drinking parents showed acute awareness of their children's hurt, although sometimes their preoccupation with drink made it hard for them to act on this remorse or convey it to their children. Information from professionals and young adults suggest that it is common for communication about the drink-related problems to be quite limited, both within the family or with outsiders. Even non-drinking parents may be reluctant to speak openly with their children about the problems, whether out of shame or a wish to protect them from harsh reality (as also happens with divorce, for instance). Conversely, children may become confidants taking on a quasi-spouse role ahead of their time.

Especially as they grew older, the children were not passive in relation to the drinking. Typically they tried to dissuade the parent from drinking or took direct action like hiding bottles. Common defence mechanisms were avoidance, externalisation (both positive and negative) and internalisation.

All the children were able to identify a confidant or support person. These were virtually all close family members - the other parent, grandparents, aunts and uncles, sisters and brothers. The majority were female, but about a third were male. This gender pattern is typical of children's network relationships (Cochrane et al., 1990).

Children in two parent households where only one parent drank heavily had the support of one sober parent during episodes of inebriation, which was not the case for children whose lone parent drank heavily or who experienced two parents drunk together. On the other hand the former could experience more adult arguments and conflict about the drinking.

When there is more than one child in the family or household, the implications can be quite different for particular children. In a number of families the oldest child at home seemed to bear the brunt of the problems. There were examples of them protecting or looking after younger children and, in adolescence, challenging the drinker's life-style or aggression. Sometimes a strong sense of solidarity amongst brothers and sisters helped them cope and be more assertive, though in other families siblings did not appear to give each other much support.

Long-term implications

The study was intended primarily to focus on the current impact of drinking. Nevertheless, interviews with older adolescents and young adults gave insights intolonger term implications. For some these had been quite dire, leading to anti-social behaviour, disenchantment with education and social isolation. In these cases, heavy drinking was often combined with other major family difficulties. On the other hand, a good number of 'survivors' appeared to be functioning well. They could even recognise gains, such as family closeness, a determination to do well or increased empathy with young people in trouble.

Children's needs and rights

The design and scale of this study was not intended to identify the extent, distribution or intensity of needs. What it can do is depict the nature of some of those needs, as perceived in part by parents and professionals, but most significantly by children themselves.

Needs and rights of children in general

Any population or group of children have *general needs and rights* which are shared with all or most other children. They may also have *specific needs and rights* which derive from their particular situation or characteristics, such as being a refugee, growing up in care, having a disability, or having a parent whose functioning is seriously affected by alcohol misuse.

Needs and rights are closely related. Needs may be identified by people themselves (passively or actively), by professionals or by experts as deficiencies or wants which can be met by others in order to achieve a sufficient quality of life, however defined (Bradshaw, 1972; Doyal and Gough, 1991). Rights can be seen as representing formal or legal claims on others to act positively in a person's interests or to desist from interfering with that person's freedom. As embodied in the UN Convention children's' rights can be broadly grouped into rights to nurturance and survival, to protection, to services and to participation (Asquith and Hill, 1994). Most of such rights can be seen as entitlements to have needs met. Significantly, there is also an entitlement to influence decisions about *how* those needs are best met.

Whilst perceptions of children's universal needs vary with culture, time and place, there is a broad consensus that in modern Britain such qualities as love, consistency, belonging, limit-setting, stimulation and opportunities for responsibility and self-fulfilment are important requirements for a satisfactory upbringing (Pringle, 1980; Woodhead, 1990; Schaffer, 1990). These do not have to be met by parents, though in our society there is more emphasis than in most cultures on parental rather than extended family responsibilities. Hence when parents are partially or wholly unable to fulfil parental responsibilities as a result of heavy drinking, they are likely to face opprobrium and risk losing some of the entitlements which are linked to parenthood. In everyday practice, the major responsibilities for physical care and domestic organisation usually rest more with women. In consequence the conflict between alcohol misuse and societal expectations about parenting may be especially great for mothers (Shucksmith, 1994).

Needs and rights of children of problem drinkers

Problem drinking alters the parent-child relationship in various ways. At least temporarily and sometimes more substantially it reduces a parent's ability to meet their child's needs and take account of their wishes and interests. One of the strong messages which comes from this and other studies is that when parents drink heavily, there can be a role reversal when the child becomes physically, psychologically or emotionally responsible in order to make up for the parent's incapacities. They may take on the care and worry work normally assumed by mothers (James, 1989; Oakley, 1995). This can lead offspring to feel they have 'lost' their childhood in some way and that the drinking biological parent has forfeited the right to be regarded and respected as a true social parent. In addition, when both parents or a lone parent drink heavily, attenuation or distance of kin contacts can mean there is no-one else close at hand willing and able to offer substitute care.

Children and young adults in this sample explicitly or implicitly identified a very wide range of needs. Admittedly a few who accepted their parents' drinking did not express any wish for change, but nearly everyone did want the drinking to stop. Taken together with their predominantly unhappy feelings about the drinking, it is clear that children's most important needs are for parents to avoid drinking so heavily that it affects their child-rearing role and for parents already in that position to be able to control their drinking. Of course, this is almost a trite conclusion and one which many individuals, agencies, professionals and policy-makers have been trying to act on for years if not centuries. Evidently there is no easy way of meeting that need. Nevertheless, it is worth reiterating that any measures to help children cope with parental alcohol misuse, however valuable, must not detract from attempts to prevent them being in that situation in the first place. It is possible that effective intervention directed at children may at least reduce the chances that they will repeat their drinking parents' behaviour.

Specific needs expressed in the study

In the study sample, the main needs expressed with respect to the children themselves related to interpersonal and social issues. It was the 'hurt on the inside', as one child put it, which required attention. They mentioned needs to talk over worries and fears, feel less isolated and gain support. Children themselves gave voice to wishes to take part in enjoyable activities, have a counsellor or engage in group work. Several identified financial needs. Some parents and young adults spoke of needs for alcohol education, though with differing emphases. Information and guidance could be directed at ensuring children do not feel responsible for their parents' drinking or promote understanding of how and why heavy drinking occurs. A few parents wanted family mediation. Most agreed it would be helpful for children to meet with others who are in the same situation or have been in the past.

There were only a few individuals interviewed in the study who indicated a need for practical help on account of the intermittent or regular shortage of money due to expenditure on drink. Similarly the need for protection from physical abuse was not commonly identified, though the literature and our interviews with professionals suggested that nevertheless these are important needs for significant numbers of children. In this and other respects, data about proportions of adults who drink heavily suggest our sample represents the tip of a huge iceberg of need.

In recent years, professionals have identified 'emotional abuse' as a category to set alongside physical abuse, neglect and sexual abuse (Department of Health, 1995; Stevenson, 1996). There are dangers in such an elastic term, which may be even more open to divergent interpretations than other forms of abuse. Nonetheless, children in our study made clear that less visible cruelty through constant denigration, criticism or threats by a drunken parent can inflict major damage on self-image and self-esteem. Children need and are entitled to protection from or compensation for such treatment.

Witnessing domestic violence (i.e. men's violence to women) was prominent in our sample. Domestic violence does now receive serious attention after a long period when it was largely ignored or trivialised. However, the question of its impact on children has only recently begun to be addressed (Mullender and Morley, 1994). Women's Aid has sought to help children in refuges for many years now, but few other agencies have given this issue priority. Since only one of the families in the present study had been to any kind of refuge, it is clearly important to consider how children present during domestic violence at home can be helped, along with the direct victim (usually their mother).

Existing resources

It was clear that most children in the study did have personal and external resources they were drawing on. There were also kernels of specialist services, whose skills and experience could form the basis for future development.

Informal supports

First and foremost, children's families and informal networks were providing important support functions, including advice, reassurance, compensatory activities and care. The non-drinking parent and in most instances the drinking parent when sober were usually managing to keep the families functioning except at times of crisis. Relatives and friends also provided help and advice. Educational and supportive services should clearly aim to co-operate with and enhance these informal supports wherever possible. These are the people children are spending most of their time with. With guidance and information, provided individually or collectively, they are in the best position to assist.

Organised services

Yet some children will not have such support and anyway in many families it was recognised that there were additional needs best met by outsiders - either trained personnel or 'survivors' i.e. adults who have experienced similar situations. We found too that there were a few examples of local projects showing how external help can be provided. These used a range of methods (particularly group work, individual counselling and health promotion). Several encountered difficulties in reaching the target population (adults and children). Our own research recruitment indicates that there may be a particular difficulty in engaging teenage boys.

These developments appeared isolated from each other. In some ways that is an appropriate localised response, but for an innovative service tackling such a widespread problem there could be benefits in establishing networks to share ideas and co-ordinate development.

Existing services and educational material for children appeared to be based on a common approach involving guilt-reduction, problem-management and compensatory activities. Whilst the received wisdom about tackling self-blame is laudable in terms of promoting children's positive emotions and assigning responsibilities appropriately to adults, there are dangers that this message reinforces a sense of helplessness in the children. It may also devalue the varied and often sophisticated understandings of the situation which many children have. Only a minority of children in our study expressed guilt, but they were nearly all clear they wanted to be involved in doing something about the drinking and its consequences. Any strategy for children should enable them to participate in defining the issues and the nature of the problem. It is possible that current educational approaches and instructional group work may be too top down and not take sufficient account of children's own varied perspectives. Clearly empowerment involves a difficult balance between enhancing children's knowledge and awareness, without imposing a single (adult) perspective. The experiences of adult drinkers shows that a definite coherent philosophy appeals to some people, but not others.

Options for resource development

General considerations

The families and professionals involved in the study confirmed the message of Velleman (1993a) that most children of heavy drinking parents need help. Yet any service response should take account of three factors which preclude making a simple blueprint for action:

- children's needs may vary and alter depending on a range of factors, including their age, gender, personality, family composition, nature and phase of the drinking pattern, presence or absence of other problems like poverty.

- many children are reluctant to be singled out as needing help

- there are a number of possible 'access points' where children might be encouraged to learn about and make use of assistance (e.g. schools, clubs, alcohol agencies, family organisations)

As a multiplicity of needs, suggestions and constraints were identified in relation to resource development, the second half of this chapter examines options and recommends guiding principles rather than proposes a single model for the way ahead.

Combined with wider knowledge from the literature and professionals, the present study identified some of the key options. It would seem that the auguries for action in the near future are good. The attention of increasing numbers of relevant professionals is turning to the issue of children's responses to parental drinking; there is now experience of a few programmes (Seilhamer and Jacob, 1990); and there has been considerable media interest (e.g. Bestic, 1994).

The sample confirmed general survey information about the extent of serious drinking and made clear that living with a parent who misuses alcohol is widespread and occurs in heterogeneous family and material circumstances. Children are affected directly and indirectly from an early age. Any strategy aimed at meeting such common, diverse and multiple needs should not focus on a single measure, but offer combinations and choices of approaches, purposes and levels of intervention. Some children who can be more readily identified and engaged will benefit from provision specifically targeted at alcohol issues, but approaches through more universal agencies like schools and youth services are needed too, in order to reach children whose problems are hidden or who are resistant to being identified as having difficulties.

The two funders of this study (the Health Education Board for Scotland and Barnardos Scotland) represented a twin interest in health education and service delivery as potential responses to the needs of children and young people in families with alcohol-related difficulties. There are several functions which these may fulfilled, alone or in combination such as:

> information-giving
> advice and guidance
> nurturance
> support
> personal insight
> empowerment

Official help may perform these functions directly, but can also assist other people to do so, including immediate family, extended family, friends and neighbours, peers, fellow survivors, teachers, other professionals, volunteers, community leaders. The level of intervention may be focused on communities (e.g. school, neighbourhood), groups, families or individuals. All this points to the need for a co-ordinating network which can act as a channel of communication, information-sharing and referral between the different parties involved in offering help in particular areas or more broadly. Councils on Alcohol could play a vital role in this respect, since they have both local branches and a national organisation.

Educational approaches

What seems to be required are a range of approaches and points of entry, which take account of children's differing stages of readiness to engage with the issues and their common feelings of stigma. There are now a number of school programmes which deal with social problems and teach appropriate coping skills. Some of these pay attention to addictions, though with a primarily preventive health education rationale. They aim to stop young people becoming heavy drinkers and mostly do not deal head on with situations where the problem is parental drinking. However, material which covers living with adults who have alcohol and other addictive problems could be incorporated into such programmes. This would in turn offer opportunities for children to refer themselves, informally and anonymously if need be, to a help line, counselling or group-based service. Primary school teachers, guidance teachers and children's rights officers have potentially key roles to play as intermediaries and disseminators, for which they would need preparation.

In the fields of health education and health promotion, the following principles have gained wide acceptance in recent years (Downie et al., 1990; Kalnins et al., 1992; Bunton et al., 1995). These are that programmes should:

- whenever possible communicate through dialogue rather than one-way imparting of current thinking

- take account of people's felt needs and priorities

- make information and advice available to the general population, as well as to targeted 'high risk' populations

Our research suggests that children affected by parental alcohol misuse already possess considerable knowledge and usually have their own ideas about causation, consequences and coping. They also demonstrated sensitive awareness of the feelings and attitudes of both family members and outsiders with regard to alcohol consumption. As indicted in Chapter 1, it is important not to underestimate the knowledge and skills of children.

It is important that any educational programme should involve sensitive dialogue wth children so that respect is shown for their competence as well as their need for understanding and reassurance. Of course, many children do not have direct experience of their parents drinking excessively. However, they too are likely to have knowledge from friends, the media and from witnessing public drunkenness. For them the benefits of involvement in a programme would derive from being better able to cope if faced with living with someone with an alcohol problem later and from reflecting on their own future drinking patterns.

Adult and community education services and libraries have a role in informing and enabling parents and people who are in touch with children, so they can respond more effectively to the children of alcohol-misusing parents and know how to refer them for specialist help. For both children and adults, clear and attractive leaflets as already provided by some Councils on Alcohol could be made available. It is important to remember that some parents themselves see a need for their children to receive outside help, either separately or with the whole family. Thus parent education and support programmes (like that pioneered by Barnardos in Northern Ireland) could provide another access route.

Services

When it comes to direct service provision, most of our respondents were in favour of facilities targeted at this particular group, although there is a case for linkage or geographical juxtaposition with other youth and family services in order to increase accessibility and reduce stigma, as Holman (1988) and Gibbons (1992) have discussed in relation to more general family services. In any case, drink-related problems are often associated or combined with other issues like poverty, separation and loss, so that any service would need to attend to other needs of children in heavy drinking families.

Location of services is also important. Especially for young children, provision needs to be quite close to home, although there is also a case for a more centralised, anonymous location. Children may benefit from specialist counselling, but many prefer to gain support from peers in the same position or from older people who have 'been through it' themselves. Often a combination is desirable. Experience suggests that a service which offers enjoyable activities as well as individual counselling and group work is likely to be most acceptable to a wide range of young people. These activities provide an incentive for attending, compensate for grim experiences at home and enable workers to build up trust before tackling social and emotional issues. Facilities should not be exclusively tailored to adolescents, since younger children need help too.

Ideally, any project should include staff or volunteers who have had experiences similar to the children's. There is scope for personal befriending services to be developed. Befrienders have been used to help young people looked after away from home or supervised by social workers (Triseliotis et al., 1995) and have been recommended for young carers (Aldridge and Becker, 1994). As noted above, any project should work in co-operation with significant members of children's network, including non-drinking parents.

The experience of this study and agencies working in this area suggest that self-referrals may be hard to attract so that active recruitment would be needed. A wide range of organisations, professionals and community projects such as those who assisted with this study could help in facilitating access to children and making the service known. Information about the service needs to be carefully worded to take account of sensitivities about identifying oneself as a child in a family with a heavy drinking parent.

As they are tilling new ground, it is important for specialist projects to be monitored or evaluated. User feedback should be a major component of that. Indeed, children's participatory rights imply that they ought to have an input to the planning processes.

A help line of some kind seems desirable to cater for children reluctant to identify themselves, for out of hours crises and as a referral point for other services. It is probably not practical to envisage a help line dedicated to this issue, so it may be more realistic for existing national and local helplines to give special attention to it. Appropriate training would assist this.

Nearly everyone in our sample could see a role for external help given directly to children themselves, but some young adults and parents saw it as important to assist family communication as well. Shared recognition of problems can help the child feel less bewildered and alone, and can establish a basis for dealing with the drinking and its effects. Whilst children have rights to be protected from undue anxiety and responsibility, they are also entitled to have a say on matters which are affecting them profoundly. Many are already well aware of the problems and keen to do something about it. The research process suggests that there is value in 'parallel' contacts with parents and children, but confidentiality would need careful handling. In his book about counselling for alcohol problems, Velleman (1992) urged his colleagues to consider offering their services to families as a whole, seeing children on their own or refering children to self-help groups. This shows again the importance of having a range of options to fit the needs and wishes of each particular child.

Although the development of programmes for children is recent and very limited, there are existing models and expertise which can be built on. It is important that developments should be responsive to local circumstances, but there is also a case for some kind of established co-ordinating mechanism so that projects can learn from each other and become aware of other options to refer individuals to if appropriate. Ideally this would also involve some young people, adult survivors and parents, who have wisdom to offer about the shaping of future initiatives.

Conclusions

The predominant impression created by the sample who took part in the study was one of diversity. Even within this limited number of cases, there was great variety in:

- the pattern of parental drinking

- children's responses, which changed over time

- the reactions and support of other family and network members

- expressed needs and views about services

These issues have to be understood within a context of changing family relationships and circumstances which may exacerbate or modify the impact of parental heavy drinking on children.

Most of the children conveyed a clear message of deep hurt resulting from parental drinking, although a minority appeared to have largely taken it in their stride. The principal problems involved verbal abuse, anxiety and uncertainty, witnessing violence and taking on adult responsibilities and 'worry work'. Although financial difficulties did figure in about a third of the families, the most common needs were for emotional support, contact with others in a similar position and more open communication. Nevertheless, many of the children seemed to be doing well in important aspects of their lives and nearly all received valued support from within the household or extended family.

Educational and service provision must take account of these differences in children's experiences and wishes, whilst giving priority to their emotional well-being. It is vital to build constructively on children's individual strengths and enhance their resourcefulness. Yet some children and young adults reported that they had limited support and social contacts. Others referred specifically to their low self-esteem and disengagement from schooling. For these particular children, it is essential to provide opportunities for social development and compensatory experiences.

The purpose of this book has been to give a voice to children brought up in the context of alcohol misuse by one or both parents. They identified a range of needs for assistance, but also illustrated strengths and supports which may help reduce or overcome the impact of excessive parental drinking. It is important that the messages we have tried to convey from and about children are heard and responded to. Alcohol agencies can become more aware of the difficulties faced by a drinker's children. Specialist agencies concerned with families, child protection, domestic violence and so on can give greater acknowledgement to the role played by drink in the particular problems they deal with. Just as important, more general purpose services like schools, family centres and youth clubs can play a pivotal role, through appropriate education, counselling and referral, in helping the children of problem drinkers to feel supported and less alone.

We have emphasised the needs of children whose parents misuse alcohol, since these have received surprisingly little focused attention. However, it is important to stress again that large surveys have shown that the majority of children in this situation go on to lead satisfactory lives. When children have good support from the other parent, relatives or even the drinking parent, they can do well. The drinking is still usually distressing, but only becomes devastating when combined with other factors, such as poverty, persistent violence or neglect.

One young man in our study thought his life had been blighted by the parental drinking, combined with the influence of the early death of his mother and physical ill-treatment by his father and stepmother. He felt this explained his life of addiction and crime which led to him being in prison at the time of the interview. By contrast, a more positive outcome is illustrated by another young adult survivor, who gained assistance from one of the organisations in our study:

> The way my Mum and Dad behaved does not have to affect my life, although it did for a long time. I don't look back and think about things 'It's all your fault because you drank'. I can look at eight out

of nine of my friends whose parents weren't heavy drinkers and they've got just the same problems that I have. I just look at it that I'm fortunate enough that my parents admitted their drinking, that I got help and that I've the skills now to address the problems that I have. In a backhanded way, I suppose I'm grateful thy had that drinking problem, because I'm able to deal with life fare better. We all have our bad days, but they don't last as long. You do get insight into how you feel. And its surprising the number of people who come to me now with their problems. And I can listen and understand.

Given support and encouragement, more children who at present 'hurt on the inside' could be helped to achieve equanimity and sensitivity like this.

References

Al-Anon Family Groups (1986) *Al-Anon Family Groups*, Al-Anon Family Groups: New York.
Alaszewski, A. and Harrison, L. (1992) 'Alcohol and social work: A literature review', *British Journal of Social Work*, Vol. 22, No. 3, pp. 331-343.
Alderson, P. (1995) *Listening to Children*, Barnardos: London.
Aldridge, J. and Becker, S. (1994) *Children who Care*, Loughborough University: Loughborough.
Aldridge, J. and Becker, S. (1994) 'The rights and wrongs of children who care', in Franklin, B. (ed.) *The Handbook of Children's Rights*, Routledge: London.
Antonovsky, A. (1987) *Unraveling the Mystery of Health*, Jossey-Bass: San Francisco.
Archard, D. (1993) *Children: Rights and Childhood*, Routledge: London.
Asquith, S. and Hill, M. (eds.) (1994) *Justice for Children*, Martinus Nijhoff: Dordrecht.
Astrop, J. (1982) *My Secret File*, Puffin: Harmondsworth.
Barbour, R. and Brown, J. (1995) *Methodological implications of a social competence model of childhood: The qualities of qualitative research?* Paper presented to the BSA Conference: University of Surrey.
Becker, J. S. (1961) *Boys in White*, University of Chicago Press: Chicago.
Belle, D. (1989) *Children's Social Networks and Social Supports*, John Wiley & Sons: New York.
Bennet, L. A. and Wolin, S. J. (1990) 'Family culture and alcohol transmission', in Collins, R. L., Leonard, K. E. and Searles, J. S. (eds.) *Alcohol and the Family*, Guilford Press: London.
Bennett, P., Murphy, S. and Smith, C. (1990) 'Health promotion and alcohol: Some sober reflections', *Health Education Journal*, Vol. 49, No. 2, pp. 80-82.
Bestic, L. (1994) 'Lives ruled by the bottle' *Independent on Sunday*, 20/11/94.

Bluebond-Langner, M. (1978) *The Private Worlds of Dying Children*, Princeton University Press: Princeton (New Jersey).

Bradshaw, J. (1972) 'The concept of social need', *New Society*, Vol. 19, pp. 640-643.

Brodzinsky, D. M., Singer, L. M. and Braff, A. M. (1984) 'Children's understanding of adoption', *Child Development*, Vol. 55, pp. 869-876.

Buckingham, D. (ed.) (1993) *Reading Audiences: Young People and the Media*, Manchester University Press: Manchester.

Bulmer, M. (1986) ed.) 'The value of qualitative research' in M. Bulmer (ed.) *Social Science and Social Policy*, Allen & Unwin: London.

Bunton, R., Nettleton, S. and Burrows, R. (1995) *The Sociology of Health Promotion*, Routledge: London.

Bury, A. (1993) *Researching Children. The same or different?* Paper presented to the BSA Conference: University of Essex.

Central Statistical Office (1994) *Social Focus on Children*, HMSO: London.

Cochrane, M., Larner, M., Riley, D. Gunnarsson, L. and Henderson, C, R. (1990) *Extending Families: The Social Networks of parents and Their Children*, Cambridge University Press: Cambridge.

Coleman, R. and Cassell, D. (1995) 'Parents who misuse drugs and alcohol', in P. Reder and C. Lucey (eds.) *Assessment of Parenting: Psychiatric and Psychological Contributions*, Routledge: London.

Collins, R. L., Leonard, K. E. and Searles, J. S. (eds.) (1990) *Alcohol and the Family*, Guilford Press: London.

Collins, S. (ed.) (1990) *Alcohol, Social Work and Helping*. Tavistock/Routledge: London.

Cox, M. V. (1980) *Are Young Childen Egocentric?*, Batsford: London.

Dallos, R. (1995) 'Constructing family life: Family belief systems' in Muncie, J., Wetherell, M., Dallos, R. and Cochrange, A. (eds.) *Understanding the Family*, Sage: London.

Davidson, G. (1992) *Problem-drinking as a factor in cases of child mistreatment*, Powys Social Services: Landrindod Wells.

Department of Health (1995) *Child Protection:Messages from Research*, Department of Health, London.

Donaldson, M. (1978) *Children's Minds*, Fontana: London.

Downie, R. S., Fyfe, C. and Tannahill, A. (1990) *Health Promotion: Models and values*, Oxford University Press: Oxford.

Doyal, L, and Gough, I. (1991) *A Theory of Human Need*, Macmillan: London.

Duncombe, J. and Marsden, D. (1995) '"Workaholics" and "Whingeing women": theorising intimacy and emotion work: the last frontier of gender equality?', *The Sociological Review*, Vol. 43, No. 1, pp. 150-169.

Dunn, J. and McGuire, S. (1992) 'Sibling and peer relationships in childhood', *Journal of Child Psychology and Psychiatry*, Vol. 33, No. 1, pp. 67-105.

Edelstein, S, B. (1995) *Children with prenatal alcohol and other drug exposure: Weighing the risks of adoption*, CWLA Press: Washington DC.

Ennew, J. (1986) *The Sexual Exploition of Children*, Blackwell: Oxford.

Ennew, J. (1994) 'Time for children or time for adults', in Qvortrup, Bardy, M., Sgritta, G. and Wintersberger, H. (eds.) *Childhood Matters*, Avebury: Aldershot.

Ernst, L. and Angst, J. (1983) *Birth Order: Its Influence on Personality* Springer Verlag: Berlin.

Fahlberg, V. (1994) 'A child's journey through placement' BAAF: London.

Fanti, G, (1990) 'Helping the family' in S. Collins (ed.) *Alcohol, Social Work and Helping*, Tavistock/Routledge: London.

Fossey, E. (1994) *Growing Up with Alcohol*, Routledge: London.

Foxcroft, D. R. and Lowe, G. (1995) 'Adolescent drinking, smoking and other substance use involvement: links with perceived family life', *Journal of Adolsescence*, Vol. 18, pp. 159-177.

Franklin, B. (ed.) (1995) *The Handbook of Children's Rights*, Routledge: London.

Furth, H. G. (1980) *The World of Grown-ups*, Elsevier: New York: .

Garbarino, J., Stott, F. M. and Erikson Institute (1992) *What Children Can Tell Us*, Jossey-Bass: San Francisco.

Garmezy, N. (1985) 'Stress-resistant children: The search for protective factors', in J. E. Stevenson (ed.) *Recent Research in Developmental Psychology*, Pergamon Press: Oxford.

Gelles, J. (1987) 'Methods for studying sensitive family topics', *Family Violence*, , Vol. 84, pp. 183-202.

Gibbons, J. (ed.) (1992) *The Children Act 1989 and Family Support: Principles into Practice*, H.M.S.O.: London.

Goddard, E. (1991) *Drinking in England and Wales in the Late 1980s*, HMSO: London.

Goodwin, D. W. (1994) *Alcohol: The Facts*, Oxford University Press: Oxford.

Greenfield, S. (1993) 'Long-term psychosocial effects of childhood exposure to parental drinking', *American Journal of Psychiatry*, Vol. 150, No. 4, pp. 608-613.

Gulbenkian Foundation Commission (1995) *Children & Violence*, Gulbenkian Foundation: London.

Hammarberg, T. (1994) 'Justice for children through the U N Convention' in Asquith, S. and Hill, M. (eds.) *Justice for Children*, Martinus Nijhoff: Dordrecht.

Heather, N. and Robertson, I. (1986) 'Is alcoholism a disease?', *New Society*, Vol. 75, No. 1208, pp. 318-320.

Hegar, R. L. (1988) 'Sibling relationships and separations: implications for child placement', *Social Service Review*, Vol. 62, pp. 446-467.

Hendrick, H. (1993) *Child Welfare: England 1872-1989*, Routledge: London.

Hill, M. (1987), *Sharing Child Care in Early Parenthood*, Routledge & Kegan Paul: London.

Hill, M., and Aldgate, J. (eds.) (1996) *Child Welfare in the United Kingdom and Ireland*, Jessica Kingsley: London.

Hill, M., Lambert, L. and Triseliotis, J. (1989) *Achieving Adoption with Love and Money*, National Children's Bureau: London.

Hill, M. and Triseliotis, J. (1990), 'Who do you think you are? Towards understanding adopted children's sense of identity', in J. Ross and V. Bergum (eds.) *Through the Looking-glass: Children and Health Promotion*, Canadian Public Health Association: Ottawa.

Holman, R. (1988) *Putting Families First*, Macmillan: London.

Jahoda, G. and Cramond, J. (1972) *Children and Alcohol*, H.M.S.O.: London.

James, A. (1993) *Childhood Identities*, Edinburgh University Press: Edinburgh.

James, A. and Prout, A. (eds.) (1990) *Constructing and Reconstructing Childhood*, Falmer Press: London.

James, N. (1989) 'Emotional labour: skill and work in the social regulation of feelings', *Sociological Review*, Vol. 37, No. 1, pp. 15-42.

Johnson, J. L. and Rolf, J. E. (1990) 'When children change: Research perspectives on children of alcoholics', in Collins, R. L., Leonard, K. E. and Searles, J. S. (eds.) Alcohol and the Family, Guilford Press: London.

Jones, D. C. and Houts, R. (1992) 'Parental drinking, parent-child communication, and social skills in young adults', *Journal of Studies on Alcohol*, Vol. 53, No. 1, pp. 48-56.

Kalnins, I., McQueen, D. V., Backett, K. C., Curtice, L. and Currie, C. A. (1992) 'Children, empowerment and health promotion: New directions in research and practice', *Health Promotion International*, Vol. 7, No. 1, pp. 53-59.

Keith, L. and Morris, J. (1995) 'Easy targets: a disability rights perspective on the 'children as carers' debate', *Critical Social Policy*, Issue 44/5, pp. 36-57.

Kosonen, M. (1994) 'Sibling relationships for children in the care system', *Adoption & Fostering*, Vol. 18, No. 3, pp. 30-35.

Krahn, G. L. (1993) 'Conceptualizing social support in families of children with special health needs', *Family Process*, Vol. 32, pp. 235-248.

LaFontaine, J. (1986) 'An anthropological perspective on children', in Richards, M. and Light, P. (eds.) *Children of Social Worlds*, Blackwell: Oxford.

Lambert, L., Buist, M., Triseliotis, J. and Hill, M. (1990) *Freeing Children For Adoption*, BAAF: London.

Le Francois, G. (1990) *The Lifespan*, Wadsworth, London.

McCord, J. (1990) 'Long-term perspectives on parental absence', in L. Robins and M. Rutter (eds.) *Straight and Deviant Pathways from Childhood to Adulthood*, Cambridge Univesity Press: Cambridge.

McCubbin, H. I., Sussman, M. B. and Patterson, J. M. (1983) *Social Stress and the Family*, Haworth Press: New York.

McGrady, B. S. and Hay, W. (1987) 'Coping with problem drinking in the family', in J. Orford (ed.) *Coping with Disorder in the Family*, Croom Helm: London.

McNamara, J. (1995) *Bruised from Birth*, BAAF: London.

Martin, F., Murray, K. and Fox, S. (1981) *Children out of Court*, Scottish Academic Press: Edinburgh.

May, C. (1991) 'Research on alcohol education for young people: a critical review of the literature', *Health Education Journal*, Vol. 50, No. 4pp. 195-199.

May, C. (1993) 'Resistance to peer group pressure: an inadequate basis for alcohol education', *Health Education Research*, Vol. 8, No. 2, pp. 159-16

Mayall, B. (1993) 'Keeping healthy at home and school: 'It's my body, so it's my job', *Sociology of Health and Illness*, Vol. 15, No. 4,pp. 464-487.

Mayall, B. (ed.) (1994) *Children's childhoods observed and experienced*, Falmer Press: London.

Miller, W. R. and Kurtz, E. (1994) 'Models of alcoholism used in treatment: Contasting AA and other perspectives with which it is often confused', *Journal of Studies on Alcohol*, Vol. 55, pp. 159-172.

Mitchell, A (1985) *Children in the Middle*, Tavistock: London

Mullender, A. and Morley, R. (eds.) *Children living with Domestic Violence: Putting Men's Abuse of Women on the Child Care Agenda*. Whiting and Birch: London.

Munro, A., Barrie, K., Carr, A. Holttum, S. Baillie, P. and Girvan, M. (1994) *Alcohol Services for Children, Young People and Families in Scotland*, University of Paisley: Paisley.

Murray-Parkes, C. (1972) *Bereavement - Studies of Grief in Adult Life*, Tavistock: London.

Nastasi, B. K. and DeZolt, D. M. (1994) *School Interventions for Children of Alcoholics*, Guilford Press: New York.

Newell, P. (1993) 'The child's right to physical integrity', *International Journal of Children's Rights*, Vol. 1, No. 1, pp. 101-104.

Newson, J. and Newson, E. (1976) *Seven Years Old in the Home Environment*, Wiley: New York.

Nicholson, J. (1984) *Men and Women*, Oxford University Press: Oxford.

Oakley, A. (1994) 'Women and children first and last: Parallels and differences between children's and women's studies', in B. Mayall (ed.) *Children's childhoods observed and experienced*, Falmer Press: London.

Orford, J. (1985) 'Alcohol problems and the family', in J. Lishman and G. Horobin (eds.) *Approaches to Addiction*, Kogan Page: London.

Orford, J. and Velleman, R. (1990) 'Offspring of parents with drink problems: drinking and drug-taking as young adults', *British Journal of Addiction*, Vol. 85,pp. 779-794.

Parton, N. (1991) *Governing the Family*, Macmillan: London.

Pringle, M. K. (1980) *The Needs of Children*, Hutchinson: London.

Quinton, D. and Rutter, M. (1988) *Parenting Breakdown*, Avebury: Aldershot.

Qvortrup, J. (1991) *Childhood as a Social Phenomenon*, Eurosocial Report Vol. 36, European Centre for Social Welfare Policy and Research, Vienna.

Qvortrup, Bardy, M., Sgritta, G. and Wintersberger, H. (eds.) (1994) *Childhood Matters*, Avebury: Aldershot

Reder, P., Duncan, S. and Gray, M. (1993) *Beyond Blame: Child Abuse Tragedies Revisited*, Routledge: London.

Redgrave, K. (1987*) Child's Play*, Boys and Girls Welfare Society: Manchester.

Reed, J. (1995) 'Young Carers', *Highlight No. 137,* National Children's Bureau: London.

Renzetti, C. M. and Raymond, M. L. (eds.) (1995) *Researching Sensitive Topics*, Sage: London.

Rheingold, H. L. (1982) 'Ethics as an integral part of research in child development', in R. Vasta (ed.) *Strategies and Techniques in Child Study*, Academic Press: New York.

Richards, M. and Light, P. (eds.) (1986) *Children of Social Worlds*, Blackwell: Oxford.

Robertson, I and Heather, N. (1992) *So you want to cut down your drinking?* HEBS: Edinburgh.

Rogers, R. S. (1992) 'The social construction of childhood' in W. S. Rogers, D. Hevey, J. Roche and E. Ash (Eds) *Child Abuse and Neglect* Batsford: London.

Roosa, M. W., Michels, M., Groppenbacher, N. and Gersen, J. (1993) 'Validity of children's reports of parental alcohol abuse', *Journal of Studies on Alcohol* Vol. 54, No. 1, pp. 71-79.

Ross, J. and Bergum, V. (eds.) (1990) *Through the Looking-glass: Children and Health Promotion*, Canadian Public Health Association: Ottawa.

Rutter, M. (1980) *Maternal Deprivation Re-assessed*, Penguin: Harmondsworth.

Rutter, M. (1985) 'Resilience in the face of adversity', *British Journal of Psychiatry*, Vol. 147, pp. 598-611.

Ryan, T. and Walker, R. (1993) *Life Story Work*, BAAF: London.

Schaffer, H. R. (1990) *Making Decisions about Children*, Blackwell: Oxford.

Seilhamer, R. A. and Jacob, T. (1990) 'Family factors and adjustment of children of alcoholics', in M. Windle and P. Searles (eds.) *Children of Alcoholics: Critical Perspectives*, Guilford: New York.

Seilhamer, R. A., Jacob, T. and Dunn, N. J. (1993) 'The impact of alcohol consumption on parent-child relationships in families of alcoholics', *Journal of Studies on Alcohol*, Vol. 54, pp. 89-198.

Sharp, C. (1994) *Alcohol Education for Young People: A Review of the Literature 1983-1993*, NFER: Slough.

Shucksmith, J. (1994) *Children, Families and Alcohol*, Report for HEBS and Barnardo's: University of Aberdeen.

Silverman, D. (1993) *Interpreting Qualitative Data*, Sage: London.

Simpson, M., Williams, B. and Kendrick, A. (1993) *Social Work Responses to the Misuse of Alcohol: A Literature Review*, Scottish Office Central Research Unit: Edinburgh.

Smith, D. (1989) 'Social work with problem drinkers', *Practice*, Vol. 4, pp. 346-357.

Solberg, A. (1990) 'Negotiating childhood: Changing constructions of age for Norwegian children', in James, A. and Prout, A. *Constructing and Reconstructing Childhood*, Falmer Press: London.

Spencer, J. R. and Flin, R. (1991) *The Evidence of Children*, Blackstone Press: London.

Stafford, D. (1992) *Children of Alcoholics*, Piatkus: London.

Stevenson, O. (1996) 'Emotional abuse', *Child and Family Social Work*, Vol. 1, No. 1

Sutton-Smith, B. and Rosenberg, M. (1970) *The Sibling*, Holt, Rinehart and Winston: New York.

Triseliotis, J., Borland, M., Hill, M. and Lambert, L. (1995) *Teenagers and the Social Work Services*, HMSO: London

Velleman, R. (1992) *Counselling for Alcohol Problems*, Sage: London.

Velleman, R. (1993a) *Alcohol and the family*, Report for the Institute of Alcohol Studies: London.

Velleman, R. (1993b) 'Parental alcohol abuse - children's experience, children's response', *Childright*, Vol. 99, pp. 11-14.

Velleman, R. (1995) 'Resilient and Un-resilient Transtion to Adulthood: The children of problem drinking parents', *Paper presented at the 'Alcohol and the Family' Conference*, Insititute of Alcohol Studies, London.

Velleman, R. and Orford, J. (1990) 'Young adult offspring of parents with drinking problems: Recollections of parents' drinking and its immediate effects', *British Journal of Clinical Psychology*, Vol. 29, pp. 297-317.

Velleman, R. and Orford, J. (1993a) 'The importance of family discord in explaining childhood problems in the children of problem drinkers', *Addiction Research*, Vol. 1, pp. 39-57.

Velleman, and Orford, J. (1993b) 'The adult adjustment of offspring of parents with drinking problems', *British Journal of Psychiatry*, Vol. 162, pp. 503-516.

Walker, R. (1985) 'Evaluating applied qualitative research', in R. Walker (ed.) *Applied Qualitative Research*, Gower: Guildford.

Weisner, T. S. and Gallimore, R. (1977) 'My brother's keeper: Child and sibling caretaking', *Current Anthropology*, Vol. 18, No. 2, pp. 169-190.

Werner, E. E. (1986) 'Resilient offspring of alcoholics: A longitudinal study from Birth to Age 18', *Journal of Studies on Alcohol*, pp. 34-40.

Woodhead, M. (1990) 'Psychology and the cultural construction of children's needs' in James, A. and Prout, A (eds.) . *Constructing and Reconstructing Childhood*, Falmer Press: London, 1990.

Woodhead, M., Light, P. and Carr, R. (eds.) (1991) *Growing up in a Changing Society*. Open University Press: Buckingham.

Woodroffe, C., Glickman, M., Barker, M. and Power, C. (1993) *Children, Teenagers and Health: The Key Facts*, Open University Press: Miltion Keynes

Youniss, J. and Smollar, J. (1985) *Adolescent relations with mothers, fathers and friends*, University of Chicago Press: Chicago.

Appendix 1

Children's interview schedule

N. B. These questions were used flexibly to explore issues with each child in a manner which suited the child's age, circumstances and wishes.

Introductory worksheet- 'my likes and dislikes'

Includes pictures, questions and requests for sentence completion on topics such as :
    My favourite colour
    My favourite film
    My favourite time of year
    The best day of my life
    What I hate doing most in the world

The child's perception and understanding of alcohol

Introduced by means of card pack.
    Is everybody allowed to drink all of these drinks?
    Have you tasted any of them?
    Did you like it?
    Where have you seen people drinking them?
    What happens to people when they drink a lot of these?
    How can you tell when somebody is drunk?

The child's perceptions of alcoholic drinking in the family

    Who are the people in your family? Who do you live with?
    Does anyone drink in your family?
    Where are you when ....is drinking?

What's ....like when s/he is not drinking?
Which do you prefer, ...when s/he is drinking or when not drinking?
What's ....like when s/he is drunk? (With use of written prompts)
How does it make you feel when .... is drunk? (With use of written and visual prompts)
Have you ever wanted to stop .... drinking?
Who do you think it's affected most in your family?
Have you ever wanted to tell anybody about it? If so, who?
Do you think you will drink when you grow up?

Service provision

Would you like to meet with other children who had the same experiences as you?
If you had the job of choosing the people to work for a Barnardo's project for children's whose parents drink, what sort of person would you choose?
What kind of person would you never give the job to?

Ending

If someone gave you three special wishes for the future what would they be?

Appendix 2

Young adults' interview schedule

N. B. This questionnaire was used with older teenagers as well as young adults. Themes were used flexibly according to the circmstances.

The drinking parents

Who is/was/were the problem drinker(s) in the family?
What form did the drinking take? [What kinds of drink, how much, where, when, who with. Steady pattern or 'binges']
What in his/er life influenced him/her to become a heavy drinker?
Who or what did you hold most responsible for the drinking?
Was the drinking parent away from home a lot? [How long, for what reasons]
Did you see the drinking as normal or unusual? Did this change as you grew older?
When did you first become aware of the drinking difficulties?
When did you realise the difference between alcoholic and non-alcoholic drinks?
How did the drinking change as you got older? [Probe about efforts to give up, relapses etc.]
How did your view of the drinking change as you grew older?
How did the parent behave when drunk? [Probe - did you witness violence? experience violence to yourself?]
How did the parent behave when not drunk?
Did you get caught up in arguments about the drink or related problems? How?
Were there many other heavy drinkers amongst your relatives, friends or neighbours?
Did your parents ask you to drink with them? From what age?

Impact of the drinking

How did you get on generally with your parent(s)?
In what ways was this different when s/he was drinking?
Did either parent's attitude to rules and discipline change when the drinking was going on?
How important was the drinking by your parent(s) as part of your whole childhood?
What were your feelings when X was drunk? How did this change as you grew older?
Was you parent sometimes fun when drunk?
What did you do when s/he was drinking heavily?
Were there things you deliberately avoided doing when your parent was drunk?
Did you do things to try and stop him/her drinking?
What worries and fears did you have? For yourself? For your parent(s)?
Did you ever feel to blame? Were you made to feel blame?
Were there times when you were left alone? Got ready for school by yourself? Had to do things like shopping or cooking at an earlier age than usual?
What skills did you develop which you might not otherwise have done?
How was your schooling affected? [Probe - tired, not concentrate, took time off]
Did it affect when and where you spent time with friends? With girlfriends or boyfriends?
Did you ever have to be looked after by someone outside the family as a result of your parent drinking too much?
What were the effects, if any, on such things as mealtimes, holidays, Christmas and New Year?
What has been your own drinking pattern? How was this affected by your parent's drinking?
What part, if any, do you think your parents drinking has had on any current difficulties in life which you may have?
How do you get on with your drinking parent now?

The non-drinking parent (if applicable)

How well did you get on with him/her?
Which parent were you closest to? [May include step-parents]
How was your relationship different when the other (drinking) parent was not there?
What was his/her attitude to the drinking?
How did this change over time?
Were there arguments or disagreements?

How did they get on, apart from the drink?
Did s/he seek to protect you from the effects of the drink? How?
Did s/he try to make up for the effects of the drink? How?
How you think the parental relationship affected the drinking?

Communication and help-seeking

How much did your parents talk to you about the drinking?
What explanations did they give?
Do you wish they had been more open? If so, in what ways?
Did they indicate it was something to be kept secret from others?
Were there people you particularly did not want to tell?
With whom did you talk about the drinking? Why did you choose to tell that person/those people?
How did people respond when you talked to them or sought help?
Amongst your relatives, friends and neighbours, who were the most helpful people to a) talk to b) help in more practical ways
What did friends of your own age think? Say?
Did you have any friends in a similar position?
Do you recall times when you felt embarrassed or ashamed? Please tell me about that.
Did you have ways of explaining (away) your Dad/Mum's behaviour to other people?
Were there times that you would have liked to talk to someone about the difficulties but were not able to? if so, what or who might have enabled you to confide?

Brothers and sisters (if applicable)

How many of you were there in the family?
How close were you as children?
Can you describe the different effects the drink had on your siblings compared with yourself?
How did their view of the drinking differ from yours?
Did you and your siblings help each other in dealing with the difficulties arising from the drink?

Contact with professionals

What help (if any) was offered or given to the drinking parent?
What attention (if any) was offered or given to you?

Did you meet with other children or young people in similar circumstances? If yes, how helpful was that. If no, do you think it would have been helpful?
Which people (if any) did you find helpful? a) for your parents b) for yourself
Which people (if any) did you find unhelpful? a) for your parents b) for yourself
What services would you like to see made available for children in families where there are drink problems?
What kind of people should run these services? [Probe on a) personal qualities or experience b) type of profession or background]
What is the best kind of location and building?

General conclusions

What have been the best things in your life?
What have been the worst things?
Who has had the most positive influence on your life? (How?)
Who has had the most negative influence? (How?)
How do you think your life might have turned out differently if your parent had not had drink problems?
What have you learned from this experience?
What would you try to do differently if/when you have children yourself?
What advice would you give to children growing up in a family where there is a drink problem?
What advice would you give to parents in this situation?

Appendix 3

Parents' interview schedule

Themes covered

Background

Family information
    parents, children, extended family nearby
Neighbourhood
    What is it like? (neighbours, school etc.)
Focus child
    What is s/he like as person?
    How does s/he spend time evenings, weekends, holidays?
    Who does s/he spend time with at mealtimes, play, watching TV, bedtimes?
    Who does s/he travels to school with, to recreational activities?
    Relationships with siblings, friends, other relatives

Drinking

Drinking patterns
    Who drinks in family? (including children)
    Who is problem drinker?
    Amount, pattern and place of "normal" and "Problem" drinking in family; how compares with neighbourhood/extended family norms
    How does drinking affect problem drinker's behaviour?
    Role of non-drinking partner

Child's awareness of what drinking is
    Awareness of drinking taking place (family secret/open)
    Is it seen as negative, positive or normal by child?

How important in child's life?
How does child talk about drinking (family language)?
Who else knows about it, cover stories, confiding?

Impact on the child

What are the effects?
Fears and worries?
Need for substitute care?
Does s/he spend time alone or without supervision?
Role reversal, housework, caring
Effects on school, concentration, play
Future influence on own drinking
Is the child drinking now?
Relationships with problem drinker, other parent, siblings; their relative importance
Identification with problem drinker
Variations in relationship when drunk/sober/absent

How does child cope if drinking is a problem for him/her
(encourage open-ended responses; only prompt if appropriate)

Self esteem, anxiety, reasoning
Denial, avoidance
Help-seeking, positive family alliances, shared responsibility, stoicism, compensatory successes
Turning to other parent, sibs, pets, toys

Social networks

What are the attitudes of relatives, friends, neighbours? Helpful or unhelpful to child?
Who does the child need to conceal from, who able to confide in?
Who offers practical help, company, support, advice?
How do these people affect the child's understanding of drinking, general and specific?

Role of agencies (social, medical)

Who is the family involved with (social work, homemakers, special units, hospital)?
Which are seen as positive/negative by child?

Which seem to offer significant support to child?
Ideas about gaps in helpful provision for children?
What shape would parent like to see Barnardo's project taking?

Ending

Who and what have been the most positive influences on child?

N. B. The interviews with professionals covered similar themes, but with more attention to service provision.

Appendix 4

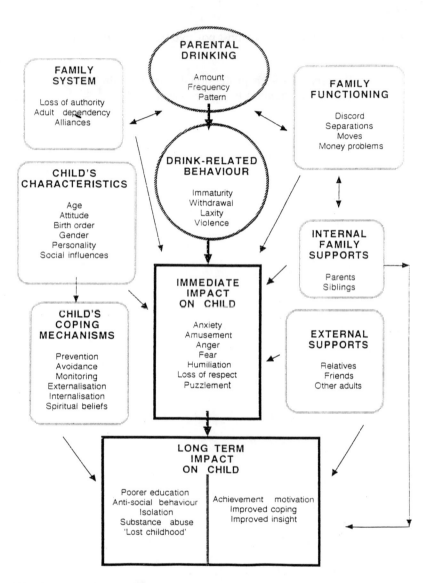

The impact of parental drinking on children

Subject index

Aberlour Child Care Trust 105-106
Abstinence 41
  (see also Total abstinence)
Access to families 20
  networking 21-22
Age as protective factor 76
Ages of respondents 22-23
Al-Anon 101
Al-Ateen 101
Alcohol agencies 101-106
Alcohol consumption
  (see also Drinking patterns)
  social attitudes 1
  children's awareness 4, 44
  children's attitudes 5, 44
  dangers of excess 2, 3
  parental levels 4
Alcoholics Anonymous 101, 102
Analysis 30-31
Anonymity 19, 31-32, 101, 112
ASK (Alcohol Support Services for Kids) 104-105
Attributions
  of reasons for parental drinking 47, 125
  of blame 68-69

Behaviour changes when drinking 38, 52
Birth order 7
Blame
  children's self-blame 46, 68-69, 103-105, 120, 125, 131

Child abuse and drinking 7
Child-centred approaches in social science 12
Childhood
  images of 13, 97-98

Child Line 109
Children
  as carers (see role reversal)
  as mediators between parents 65-66
  as objects of study 13
  as parental confidants 66
  as protectors of parents 65
  as shapers of events 13, 78-79, 117, 127
  existing knowledge and skills 117, 134
  needs for support 129-130
  perspectives 2, 11-14, 18
  rights 11, 12, 128-129
  understanding of problem drinking 44-46, 117
  views on parental drinking 3
Children's Hearings 94
Communication 9, 14
  and family secrecy 62
  as a source of support 90-92, 108
  in drinking families 90-92, 120, 127
Confidants 83-84, 86-89, 120
Confidentiality 19-20, 31-33, 112-113, 136
Controlled drinking 41
  (see also Social drinking)
Coping 43, 75-83, 119-120, 127
  by avoidance 80, 119
  by denial 119
  by direct action 78-79
  emotion-focused coping 79
  externalisation 81-83, 119
  gender differences in 80-82, 119
  influences on coping style 92
  internalisation 83
  mechanisms 7
  monitoring 80-81
  outcomes of coping styles 92
  problem focused 78-79
  pro-social strategies 81-83, 92
  and resilience 8, 75-78
  skills 98, 103-104
  social background differences 82-83
  with emotional impact of drinking 79-83
Council on Alcohol programmes 102
Counselling 105, 107, 109

Denial 20
  (see also Communication and Secrecy)

Detoxification Units 102
Divorce (see Family dislocation)
Drinking patterns of parents 36-42
  frequency 36
  gender differences 36
  location 36
  household type 36
  impact on children 59
  professionals' views 116

Education programmes on alcohol 5
Educational failure 94-95, 120
Ethical considerations in research 31-32

Family alliances 66-67
Family and Alcohol Project 106
Family dynamics 43, 62-73, 118-119
Family dislocation 57, 94
Family systems (see Family dynamics)
Financial problems 8, 57058
Friends 73, 88-89, 108, 120

GEAAP (Greater Easterhouse Alcohol and Addiction Project) 105
Gender
  children's stereotypes 5
  differences and child abuse 7
  and drinking 39, 75, 116
Grandparents 72, 87, 120
Groups for children of drinking parents 104
Guilt (see Blame)

Hangovers 59
Health services 102
Help lines 103, 109

Impact on children of problem drinking 6-7, 43-61
  emotional 43, 47-56, 116-118
  long term 43, 94-99
Informed consent 15, 31
Interviews 18-19, 123
  funnelling technique 30
  non-verbal communication 28-29, 33
  parallel interviews 27, 32
  recording 30
  with children 27-29, 33-34
  with parents 30

Interviews (ctd)
  with young adults 29-30

Lone parents 24, 37
  (see also Family dislocation)
Long term effects of parental drinking 6, 127
Lost childhood 97-98

Monitoring by children of parental drinking 78, 80-81

Networking agencies 20-22
Needs (see Children's rights)
NHS Addiction Clinics 102
Non-drinking parents 40, 52, 54, 64, 66-67, 84-85, 91
Norms about drinking 39-41, 77-78
  class differences 39, 116-117
  effects of contrasting models 40
  and family of origin 40
  gender differences 39
  and reduction of stress 78, 116-117
  in rural areas 39-40

Parental authority, loss of 69-71
Parental laxity 94-95, 120
Parental problem drinking
  difficulty in defining 3-4
  effects on children 2
  extent of 3
  feelings of guilt 69
  negative effects 38, 50-56, 94-98, 126
  positive effects 7, 9, 38, 47-49, 98-99, 126
  neutral effects 49-50
Peer relationships 73
  (see also Friends)
Personality as protective factor 76-77
Poverty 39, 95, 117
Problem behaviour 95, 120
Professionals
  family suspicion of 73, 111-112, 121
  perspectives on children with drinking parents 115-122
Protective factors in resisting stress 8

Recovery from problem drinking 41
  impact on children 58-60, 118-119
  support during 102

Research
  brief 10, 123
  design 16-19, 123
  with children 14
Resource development options 132-136
Rights (see Children's rights)
Role models 95, 120
Role reversal 63, 118

Salience of parental drinking for children 60, 125
Sample 17-18, 123
  bias 22, 24, 25-27, 82, 118, 124
  characteristics 22-27, 30
  self-selection 30
SCAD (Support for Children of Adult Drinkers) 103-104
School 81-82, 94, 117-120, 133
Scottish Office, The 106
Secrecy among drinking families 71-73, 96, 118
Separation (see Family dislocation)
Services for adult drinkers 9, 100-102
Services for children of drinkers 9, 100-102, 103-106, 121-122, 131
  activity groups 104-105
  befriending 104
  closed groups of survivors 103-105, 108, 110
  coordination 136
  counselling 105, 107, 109
  desired by families 104-106
  dilemmas concerning 110-113
  drop-in centres 107, 122
  education programmes 105, 109, 133-135
  evaluation 135
  family mediation 108
  help lines 103, 109, 135
  identification of 111
  independence of 110, 121
  links with other services 111
  location of 110, 135
  recruitment 112-113, 124, 135
  school-based programmes 113, 115, 122, 133
Siblings
  interviews with 28, 33
  as supports 77
Sobering up, effects of 39
Social construction of childhood 13

Social drinking
  agencies 102
  treatment models 100, 102
Social isolation of children 73, 83, 95-96, 120
Social work
  addiction units 102
  limits on confidentiality 31-32
  services for children with drinking parents 104, 106, 111-112
Stauros 101-102
Substance abuse 96-97
Supports for children 83-90, 119-120, 130-131
  (see also Services)
  extended family 83, 87, 120
  friends 88-89, 120
  grandparents 83, 87-88, 120
  informal 83-88
  parents 83-85
  peers 108
  professional 83, 89
  siblings 85-87, 120
  teachers 120
Support, spiritual 89-90, 101-102
Systems model of families (see Family dynamics)

Teachers 120
Total abstinence
  organisations 101-102
  treatment models 100-102
Triangulation, value of 32-33, 67

Verbal abuse 9, 56, 118, 126, 130
Violence 38- 53-56, 95, 117, 126, 130

UN Convention on the Rights of the Child 98

Young adults
  interviews 29-30
  recollections 33

Author index

Alaszewksi, A. 9
Alderson, P. 15
Aldgate, J. 12
Aldridge, J. 21, 63, 135
Antonovsky, A. 76, 125
Archard, D. 11
Asquith, S. 11, 128
Astrop, J. 14

Barbour, R. 14
Becker, J. S. 31
Becker, S. 63, 135
Belle, D. 10
Bennet, L.A. 5
Bennet, P. 5
Bergum, V. 63
Bestic, L. 132
Bluebond-Langner, M. 14
Bradshaw, J. 128
Brodzinsky, D.M. 12
Brown, J. 14
Buckingham, D. 14
Bulmer, M. 25
Bunton, R. 133
Bury, A. 14

Cassel, D. 7
Central Statistical Office 5
Cochrane, M. 10, 127
Coleman, R. 7
Collins, S. 9
Commission on Violence 3, 126
Cox, M.V. 13
Cramond, J. 4, 15

Dallos, R. 62
Davidson, G. 7
Department of Health 130
Dezolt, D.M. 6
Donaldson, G. 13
Downie, R.S. 133
Doyal, L. 128
Duncombe, J. 82

Edelstein, S.B. 6
Ennew, J. 13, 14, 97

Fahlberg, V. 49
Fanti, G. 7, 62
Flin, R. 12
Fossey, E. 5, 15, 44, 96
Foxcroft, D.R. 6
Franklin, B. 11
Furth, H.G. 13

Gallimore, R. 63
Garbarino, J. 14, 19, 34
Garmezy, N. 76
Gelles, J. 30
Gibbons, J. 134
Goddard, E. 4
Goodwin, D.W. 9
Gough, I. 128
Greenfield, S. 8
Gulbenkian Foundation Commission 3, 126

Hammarberg, T. 12
Harrison, L. 9
Hather, N. 3, 102
Hegar, R.L. 85
Hendrick, H. 12
Hill, M. 11, 12, 15, 19, 60, 90, 128
Holman, R. 107, 134
Houts, R. 9

Jacob, T. 132
Jahoda, G. 4, 15
James, A. 13, 14, 75
James, N. 129
Johnson, J. L. 7
Jones, D.C. 9

Kalnins, I. 133
Keith, L. 63
Kosonen, M. 85
Krahn, G.L. 125
Kurtz, E. 101

LaFontaine, J. 13, 75
Lambert, L. 7
LeFranois, G. 75
Light, P. 13
Lowe, G. 6

Marsden, D. 82
Martin, F. 94
May, C. 5
Mayall, B. 13, 14, 75
McCord, J. 8
McCubbin, H.I. 125
McGuire, S. 77
McNamara, J. 6
Miller, W.R. 5, 101
Mitchell, A. 12, 90
Morley, R. 130
Morris, J. 63
Mullender, A. 130
Munro, A. 9
Murray-Parkes, C. 33

Nastasi, B. K. 6
Newell, P. 126
Newson, E. 126
Newson, J. 126
Nicholson, J. 82

Oakley, A. 129
Orford, J. 7,8,9,24,36,62,98

Parton, N. 12
Pringle, M.K. 128
Prout, A. 13, 14, 75

Quinton, D. 82
Qvortrup, J. 3, 13, 97

Raymond, M.L. 16
Reder, P. 7
Redgrave, K. 14
Reed, J. 63
Renzetti, C.M. 16
Rheingold, H.J. 15
Richards, M. 13
Robertson, R. 3, 102
Rogers, R.S.13
Rolf, J.E. 7
Roosa, M.W. 5
Ross, J. 63
Rutter, M. 8, 76, 82
Ryan, T. 14

Schaffer, H.R. 8, 82, 128
Seilhamer, R.A. 37, 132
Sharp, C. 5, 6
Shucksmith, J. 2, 4, 9, 10, 40, 128
Silverman, D. 30
Simpson, M. 6, 7, 126
Smith, D. 102
Smollar, J. 83
Solberg, A. 14
Spencer, J.R. 12
Stafford, D. 8
Stevenson, O. 130

Triseliotis, J. 15, 135

Velleman, R. 2,3,6,7,8,9,24,36,46,69,73,98, 101, 103, 136

Walker, R. 14, 30
Weisner, T.S. 63
Werner, E.E. 8, 76
Wollin, S.J. 5
Woodhead, M. N. 13, 128
Woodroffe, C. 5

Youniss, J. 83